D1248118

THE GUY'S RULES:

A Guidebook for Married Men

Twelve Devotions for Men to Build a Better Marriage

Michael A. Burner, Jr.

THE GUYS RULES:
A GUIDEBOOK FOR MARRIED MEN

by Michael A. Burner, Jr.

© 2019 Michael A. Burner, Jr. All rights reserved.

Unless Otherwise indicated, all Scriptures are from the Holy Bible, English Standard Version, copyright © 2001, 2007, 2011, 2016 by Crossway Bibles, a division of Good News Publishers. Used by permission. All rights reserved.

Scripture quotations marked (NLT) are taken from the Holy Bible, New Living Translation, copyright © 1996, 2004, 2007. Used by permission of Tyndale House Publishers Inc., Carol Stream, Illinois 60188. All rights reserved.

Scripture marked (MSG) are taken from The Message. Copyright © 1993, 1994, 1995, 1996, 2000, 2001, 2002. Used by permission of NavPress Publishing Group.

Scripture quotations marked (AMP) are taken from the Amplified® Bible, Copyright © 2015 by The Lockman Foundation

Without limiting the rights under copyright reserved above, no part of this publication — whether in printed or ebook format, or any other published derivation — may be reproduced, stored in or introduced into a retrieval system, or transmitted, in any form or by any means (electronic, mechanical, photocopying, recording or otherwise), without the prior written permission of the publisher.

The scanning, uploading, and distribution of this book via the Internet or via any other means without the permission of the publisher is illegal and punishable by law. Please purchase only authorized electronic editions and do not participate in or encourage electronic piracy of copyrightable materials.

Published by:

LAMP POST
publishers
SPRING VALLEY · CALIFORNIA

www.lamppostpublishers.com

Trade Paperback:	ISBN-13 # 978-1-60039-241-2
ebook:	ISBN-13 # 978-1-60039-747-9

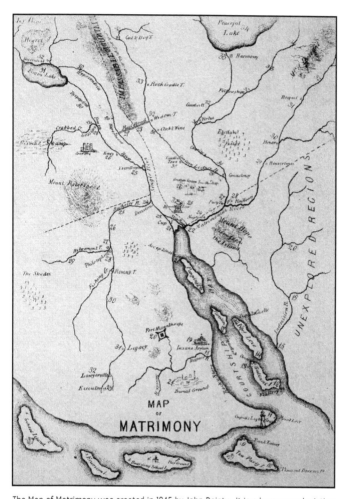

MAP
OF
MATRIMONY

The Map of Matrimony was created in 1845 by John Dainty. It is a humorous depiction of the various stages of the married life, including such locations as Courtship, Flattery Point, Cupid's Castle, Mount Respect, the icy region of Regret, Lawyerville, and an Insane Asylum alongside Despair River.

CONTENTS

FOREWORD

Have you ever started something, expecting it to be of little consequence, and then it explodes into something bigger? *The Guys Rules* was just such a project for me. As a graduation requirement to receive my Master of Theological Studies graduate degree, I was required to write a thesis paper about something from my area of study – mine was Biblical Counseling. I thought to myself, "It is better to write about what I know" – and I know my marriage and what has worked well for me. After all, I had twenty-nine years of marriage experiences and life lessons to draw upon at the time when I originally wrote the paper.

As I often did in seminary, I asked friends and family to review the paper; as Proverbs 11:14b says, "[I]n an abundance of counselors there is safety." My children, who are now adults, said, "I have heard you say all these things before." Friends said: "This is convicting," "I couldn't read this all in one sitting...I needed to chew on it," "Wow, I really need to work on my part!" and, "This is hard, but I know it is right." One friend used it as a devotional for his men's Bible study group; the resounding comment from them was, "I wish someone had told me these things early in my marriage." Another friend, in his usual honesty, said, "I don't know if I could do this. I guess I will just have to settle on being a mediocre husband." I know he did not mean it, but it gives you an idea of how challenging the concepts are. On the whole, the responses were overwhelmingly positive, and I was encouraged to share *The Guys Rules* with others.

So, unlike most every other project from seminary which I fully expected to be filed away forever, this one grew wings. I sent it to my brother, Brett, who is also an editor and publisher, to get his opinion. He encouraged me to make it into a study and add application questions. He edited it, added a few things himself, and helped put it to print. I am sure this would not have happened without his help.

When I was a Marine, I had the *Guidebook for Marines*; for husbands, I now introduce to you *The Guys Rules: A Guidebook for Married Men*. In this study are guidelines I learned the hard way. I am confident that if you implement these principles you will better your marriage and your life. *The Guys Rules* are principle and biblically based, therefore they apply to all marriages. I encourage you to go through them slowly – maybe a chapter a week – chew on the concepts, and then complete the applications following each rule. Furthermore, I strongly suggest you go through this study with other men in a similar situation (a.k.a. married), so that you can hold each other accountable and share your experiences. As Solomon says, "Iron sharpens iron, and one man sharpens another" (Proverbs 27:17).

I cannot stress the importance of completing the "Going the Extra Mile" applications at the end of each rule. Not only is there additional content supporting the rule, but you really cannot expect positive change from this study unless you apply its principles. Remember what Jesus said in Matthew 5:41b: "[I]f anyone forces you to go one mile, go with him two miles." Thus, go the extra mile; you will not regret it.

I pray that the *Guy's Rules: A Guidebook for Married Men* will positively impact your walk with the Lord and your continued journey of marriage. As you study this material, consider how blessed we are as husbands, being reminded that, "He who finds a wife finds a good thing and obtains favor from the Lord" (Proverbs 18:32).

INTRODUCTION

Did you ever wish there were a set of rules which men could follow to be a good husband and please their wives? I am a guy. I prefer that you simply write what I need to know in crayon. Have you heard of the KISS Principle... *Keep It Simple Stupid?* If you can keep it short and simple, there is a pretty good chance that what you want will be done exactly the way you want. Do not make me guess or try to read your mind. Please do not say, "If you really cared, you would know what to do!" Really?

Well, I am here to help you. These are *The Guy's Rules: A Guidebook for Married Men*, in crayon...rules which I had to learn the hard way. It took blood, sweat, and tears – a lot of them. But, after twenty-nine years of marriage and God's leading, I could not help but learn the rules that worked, and they are all biblical principles. Go figure! God's eternal Word enabled me to have a better marriage. I expect it will help yours too.

This is not a study directly about marriage, nor roles in marriage; it is not about being a father, though these things are all dealt with indirectly. *The Guys Rules* is about you walking with the Lord while taking ownership and responsibility as the leader in your marriage to your wife. You are *not* a victim, so do not act or feel like one – *do* something about it. This study will help you behave and act more effectively versus beating the air.[1]

God established Himself as the foundation of marriage. It is one of the Creation Ordinances.[2] God made man the leader of the household and the woman was made for him, and to complete him (Genesis 2:18-25, Ephesians 5:22-33). If you do not understand this, then I expect *The Guy's Rules* will not help you. If you do believe this, then I promise you, if you apply the principles contained in *The Guys Rules*, you will have a better marriage and more joy in your life.

---

1   1 Corinthians 9:26. "So I do not run aimlessly; I do not box as one beating the air."
2   The Creation Ordinances are a doctrine concerning the principles God established in Genesis 1-2. It is common for biblical scholars to list four: 1. Rest (Sabbath), 2. Work, 3. Procreation/Subdue the Earth, and 4. Marriage.

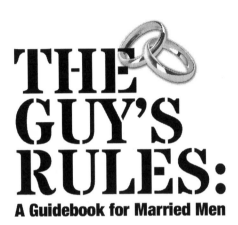

THE GUY'S RULES:

A Guidebook for Married Men

RULE ZERO:

PAGAN GUYS RULES

Everyone did what was right in his own eyes.
Judges 21:25b

There is a reason this is RULE ZERO: It adds no value. It will not help you. It is useless. Unfortunately, Rule ZERO is the most common rule husbands follow. By nature, we are selfish and put ourselves first. Below are some of what I call the *Pagan* Guy's Rules which I received in an email years ago from an anonymous source.

- Learn to work the toilet seat. You're a big girl. If it's up, put it down. We need it up, you need it down. You don't hear us complaining about you leaving it down.

- Sunday sports. It's like the full moon or the changing of the tides. Let it be.

- Crying is blackmail.

- Shopping is NOT a sport. And no, we are never going to think of it that way.

- Ask for what you want. Let us be clear on this one: Subtle hints do not work! Strong hints do not work! Obvious hints do not work! Just say it!

3

- Yes and No are perfectly acceptable answers to almost any question.

- Come to us with a problem only if you want help solving it. That's what we do. Sympathy is what your girlfriends are for.

- Anything that we said six months ago is inadmissible in an argument. In fact, all comments become null and void after seven days.

- If something we said can be interpreted two ways and one of the ways makes you sad or angry, we meant it the other way.

- If you ask a question you don't want the answer to, expect an answer that you don't want to hear.

- When we have to go somewhere, absolutely anything you wear is fine...really.

- If we ask what is wrong and you say "nothing", we will act like nothing's wrong. We know that you are lying, but it is just not worth the hassle.

- You can either ask us to do something or tell us how you want it done. Not both. If you already know how best to do it, just do it yourself.

- Christopher Columbus did not need directions and neither do we.

- Don't ask us what we're thinking about unless you are prepared to discuss such topics as baseball, the shotgun formation, or monster trucks.

Now how long do you think a guy with this attitude would last in a marriage? I doubt it would be very long. The Apostle Paul says that people who live like this are "by nature children of wrath."[3] Solomon says in Proverbs 14:12 and again in 16:25, "There is a way that seems right to a man, but its end is the way to death." I wonder why he repeats himself?

> **"When in doubt, don't."**
> *Benjamin Franklin.*
> This applies to so many things in life. If that little voice is telling you NOT to do it, you probably shouldn't. This especially applies to words. Proverbs 28:19 says, "A brother [especially a wife] offended is more unyielding than a strong city, and quarreling is like the bars of a castle." How true. However, think about what Proverbs 17:27-28 says about saying nothing, "Whoever restrains his words has knowledge, and he who has a cool spirit is a man of understanding. Even a fool who keeps silent is considered wise; when he closes his lips, he is deemed intelligent." When in doubt, say nothing!

One example of this comes from my own personal experience early in my marriage. I viewed my home as my sanctuary. Not consciously, but I was "lazy" with the effort I put out when I arrived home. My wife would have called it "selfish," but I liked my euphemism better...after all, it helped me better justify my sin. All day long at work I would be careful about what and how I communicated.

---

3   Ephesians 2:3. "...among whom we all once lived in the passions of our flesh, carrying out the desires of the body and the mind, and were by nature children of wrath, like the rest of mankind."

I was very careful about how I treated people; "my game was on" to be effective and successful. I learned early in my career that everything we do or say, or do not do or say, can have a lasting effect. I understood that, "While no single conversation is guaranteed to change the trajectory of a career, a company, a relationship or a life—any single conversation can."[4]

As you probably know, guarding your speech and actions takes a lot of conscious effort.[5] However, when I got home I would literally turn my brain off. Home was my castle and I was king. I acted as if I could say anything I wanted or thought, and not worry about how it impacted my wife or my children. After all, they loved me unconditionally. In short, I took them for granted. Consequently, around my wife, every word would just go from my brain to the air with no filter. Well, the filter was off until my wife got irritated with me – which was often; I wondered why my wife was "always" mad at me. I thought she was supposed to love me with agape love and accept me for who I was no matter what I did (Romans 15:7)[6]. I thought I was supposed to "keep it real" with my wife. I realized, and not soon enough, that my actions demonstrated I was loving those at work more than I was loving her. "Love is what love does"[7] and I was not doing love. I was honoring those at work more than

4   Susan Scott, *Fierce Conversations* (New York, NY: The Berkley Publishing Co., 2004), xix.

5   James 3:1-12.

6   Romans 15:7 (NLT). "Therefore, accept each other just as Christ has accepted you so that God will be given glory."

7   James C. Hunter, *The Servant* (New York, NY: Crown Business, 2012), 87.

the person I loved more than anyone else in the world. How did that even make sense?

Instead, I learned I needed to "take every thought captive" as it says in 2 Corinthians 10:5. Romans 12:2 tells us "not be conformed to this world, but be transformed by the renewal of your mind, that by testing you may discern what is the will of God, what is good and acceptable and perfect." Thus, I realized I needed to focus on controlling my thought life.

Rule ZERO is diametrically opposed to the will of God. What is the will of God? The Bible calls us to put others first. Jesus said, "If anyone would be first, he must be last of all and servant of all" (Mark 9:35b). We are exhorted in 1 Corinthians 10:24, "Let no one seek his own good, but the good of his neighbor." I would think our wives are the ultimate neighbor. Then in Philippians 2:4, Paul says, "Let each of you look not only to his own interests, but also to the interests of others." This takes effort and purpose. However, those we love, the most important people in our lives, are counting on us. Susan Scott, in her book *Fierce Conversations,* encourages us to "take responsibility for your emotional wake."

> For the leader [the husband], there is no trivial comment. Something you don't remember saying may have had a devastating impact on someone [your wife and children] who looked to you for guidance and approval. The conversation is not about the relationship; the conversation is the relationship.

Learning to deliver the message without the load allows you to speak with clarity, conviction, and compassion.[8]

The ten rules in this study will help you follow the will of God, love your wife, and ultimately create a better marriage. It is up to you; your wife and children are counting on you to own it. Will you?

GOING THE EXTRA MILE

1. Scriptures:
   a. Guarding your tongue: Proverbs 10:9; 12:15-16, 18, 28; 17:27-28; 21:23; Psalm 141:3; Ephesians 4:29; Colossians 4:6; James 3:1-12.
   b. Putting others first: Leviticus 19:18; Mark 12:31; Romans 12:10; Galatians 5:13; Philippians 2:3-4.

2. How could you put your wife's needs – not wants – ahead of yours when you get home from work? I would recommend you ask her; after all, her perception is more important than yours in this matter anyway. Determine the three most impactful responses and then decide what you are SPECIFICALLY going to do to address these.

3. Think about the words you use toward or say to your wife. Are they constructive? Do they build her up or edify her?[9] Do they make her feel valued? What about your actions, your tone, and your body

---

8 Scott, *Fierce Conversations*, xvi.
9 1 Corinthians 14:26b. "Let all things be done for building up."

language – after all, these are more impactful than words. Are they communicating love and that you are excited to see her? Come up with three specific things you can do to better communicate love to your wife in both word and deed, and then come up with a plan to do them. One example: When I come home, I strive to look for something SPECIFIC my wife did around the house to make it better, cleaner, or just keeping it from falling apart. Look hard for what she did and SPECIFICALLY thank her for it.

IN THE BEGINNING, GOD...

In the beginning, God...
Genesis 1:1a

"In the beginning, God..." He started this way and so must we! He must be the beginning of all things, including marriage. The first commandment tells us, "You shall have no other gods before me" (Exodus 20:3). That means God must be first; everything else comes later. Yes, your wife comes later, your kids come later, and your job comes later. Jesus tells us that the greatest commandment is to "love the Lord your God with all your heart and with all your soul and with all your mind" (Matthew 22:36b). He also says, "[W]here your treasure is, there your heart will be also. No one can serve two masters, for either he will hate the one and love the other, or he will be devoted to the one and despise the other" (Matthew 6:21, 24b). If God is not first, we will ultimately despise Him, and that is just not a good place to be. This also means that if we try to put our wives first, we will lose: it is a form of idolatry.

To have the best marriage possible, both spouses *must* put the Lord first. You cannot *make* your wife do anything, but you can 100% own your part. You can love the Lord first and make Him the beginning of all things. If you do this, and your wife is a believer, you will become the man she desires and deserves. As my wife always says to my daughter, "You must find a husband that loves the Lord more than he loves you." Be that man!

First, you need to focus on your vertical relationship and then pray for your horizontal one. This takes effort and purpose of heart – it does not just happen. One thing I have found useful is having a daily Bible reading plan. As a practice, I share these plans with my wife and children, so we are all reading the same passages together, and then we can discuss what the Lord is teaching us at the dinner table or during family devotions.

The primary benefit I have found from a reading plan is that it forces me to have a quiet time with the Lord daily. I am good at keeping personal commitments and schedules, so this practice helps me immensely. I can tell you that *every* time I have gone off a reading plan, the next thing you know I have gone days without having time with my Lord. You can imagine the results. Jesus said, "If you abide in my word, you are truly my disciples, and you will know the truth, and the truth will set you free."[10]

Second, it is necessary for you to ensure you are getting regular fellowship with other believers. Hebrews 10:24-25 says:

---

10 John 8:31b-32.

…let us consider [thoughtfully] how we may encourage one another to love and to do good deeds, not forsaking our meeting together [as believers for worship and instruction], as is the habit of some, but encouraging one another; and all the more [faithfully] as you see the day [of Christ's return] approaching. (AMP)

As husbands, we *must* be engaged in relationships with other mature men of faith. Obviously, attending church is paramount to accomplish this, but that is only a start. There is an old saying regarding the typical bacon and eggs breakfast: "The chicken was involved but the pig was committed." We need to be committed to our local church, and not by simply warming a pew for a few hours a week. For too many people, going to church means popping in and out of the service with little or no engagement with others, before, during, and after service each week. Others say, "I don't get anything from church." I can tell you, if you are going to church to "get" anything other than God then you are going for the wrong reason.[11] I would argue you will always be disappointed if you are going to church for any other purpose. Paul exhorts us to "…let all things be done

---

11 In John Piper's book, *The Dangerous Duty of Delight*, a must-read by the way, he argues that every Christian should seek lasting pleasure and joy in the Lord. He calls this Christian hedonism. However, too many people are "far too easily pleased" as C.S. Lewis says, being momentarily satisfied with temporary pleasure and therefore quickly and easily dissatisfied with the church and ever ready to move to the next whim or fad, missing the true everlasting joy than comes from delighting and being satisfied in Him.

for building up"[12] and to use our gifts for "the common good."[13] We should be going deeper and serve at church; this is where the quality relationships are and where real fellowship thrives. It does not matter which ministry; it could be setting up for church service or cleaning up afterwards. The point is, get engaged in serving at church. Understand, there is always something constructive that needs to be done at church which you can fit into your schedule; if you cannot find it, you are not looking very hard. In general, every church has teams that focus on meeting the needs of the body, whether it is sound ministry, building maintenance, technology needs like building or managing websites, managing finances, mentoring, or even making the bulletin…every church has a group you can connect and serve together with.

Be the Spiritual Leader in your Marriage.

Let's be clear, husbands, it is your job to lead your wife, this especially applies to spiritual things. No more excuses. It should be you that ensures that you pray and read the Bible together, and both don't forsake the fellowship (Hebrews 10:25). If the Lord is truly first in your life, your life should reflect it (Matthew 7:16). Do something about it…live it!

Another thing I have discovered is that it is of critical importance to be actively engaged in discipleship or

---

12 1 Corinthians 14:26b.
13 1 Corinthians 12:7b.

mentoring. Jesus' last imperative was to "make disciples,"[14] so one way or another we must be engaged in discipleship. It is not an option. If you are young in the faith, seek out a man who you know has a great relationship with the Lord, has a great marriage, and has been married a long time with children. If you are an older more mature Christian, be available to the younger husbands; if you know someone who is struggling and you can help them, you can ask them to meet for coffee or something. Over the years, I have grown in my own relationship with the Lord through being mentored, and by personally mentoring others.

Often, having the time to meet is difficult. However, discipleship is important enough to ensure you make the time. On occasion, I have done this before work, even before the sun has come up. Saturday or Sunday mornings are also an appropriate time, before the family starts moving so as not to impact them. What has really worked well for me is multitasking in discipleship – doing something I enjoy while discipling another brother. For example, much of my discipleship has been done in conjunction with mountain biking. We drive to a trail and we talk, while on the trail we talk, then we drive home and clean up the bikes and talk. All this time is engaging in discipleship. Think about it, you can do discipleship during almost any activity you love. Maybe it is working on cars, watching or playing a sport you both love, going

---

14 Matthew 28:19.

surfing or golfing, or helping with a home improvement project. Your time is valuable, so this way you can "kill two birds with one stone," while both of you grow in the Lord and build each other up. My personal experience is that wives actually encourage this type of multitasking discipleship; they understand that it ultimately benefits them, too – this is a WIN-WIN-WIN.

I expect you would agree that it is much better to learn from the mistakes and successes of others versus having to figure it out on your own. As Solomon said, "[T]here is nothing new under the sun."[15] There probably is not much your more mature brothers in the Lord have not experienced – so, rely on them.

Lastly, this already has been implied but now I will spell it out: One of the most important tasks of a married man is to disciple his wife, to be the spiritual leader of the relationship. This is probably the most common complaint from Christian women about their husbands. They want and need to be led to the Lord, to have the Lord first in their marriage. Our job as husbands is to be a model they can imitate; as Paul said in 1 Corinthians 11:1, "Be imitators of me, as I am of Christ." The Lord must be the beginning of all things in your life. "And whatever you do [as a husband], in word or deed do everything in the name of the Lord Jesus, giving thanks to God the Father through him."[16]

---

15 Ecclesiastes 1:9.
16 Colossians 3:17.

GOING THE EXTRA MILE

1. Scriptures:

    a. Putting the Lord First: Proverbs 3:1-12; Matthew 6:31-33; John 15:5; Romans 8:5; 1 Corinthians 7:3-5; Colossians 3:1-4.

    b. Discipleship: Proverbs 27:17; Luke 6:40; 2 Timothy 2:2, 20-21; 3:16-17; Titus 2:1-8.

    c. "Follow Me": Matthew 4:19; 8:22; 9:9; 10:38; 16:24; 19:21, 28; Mark 1:17; 2:14; 10:21; Luke 5:27; 9:59; 18:22; John 1:43; 8:12; 10:27; 21:19.

2. Consider the Scriptures above and think about how many times Jesus asked people to "follow Me." How could you better follow our Lord Jesus?

3. Matthew 6:21 says "...where your treasure is, there your heart will be also." What is your treasure? Is it in a godly place? Think of one "treasure" in your life that should change, a treasure which, if eliminated, would put your heart in a better place? Share this with someone to hold you accountable and help you change it.

4. Engage in discipleship. Either find someone you could mentor or who you could be mentored by.

5. Read or listen to *Sacred Marriage*[17] by Gary L. Thomas. This should be required by every married couple. It is about putting God first in your marriage. He discusses that marriage is about service and our sanctification, and not about the pursuit of happiness.

---

17 Gary L. Thomas, Sacred Marriage (Grand Rapids, MI: Zondervan, 2015).

6. *Practicing His Presence*[18] is something we should strive to do throughout our day. I am sure you have heard people say that your relationship with the Lord must be more than attending services on Sunday mornings, therefore you must do daily devotions. I would argue, in the same manner, if your relationship with God is only 15 minutes per day, that is not a relationship. We are exhorted in 1 Thessalonians 5:17 to "pray without ceasing." The idea of this is to be in communion with the Lord continually. Think about how Nehemiah, while in the middle of a conversation with King Artaxerxes, prayed to the Lord[19], who knows our intimate thoughts[20], as he casted his cares upon Him[21]. In the same way, if you desire to put the Lord first in your life, commit to engage with the Lord throughout the day. I am not saying that I have this down, but it is my aim. I have found the book, *Practicing His Presence*[22], by Brother Lawrence and Frank Laubach, a helpful, and frankly convicting, tool to help do this. I encourage you commit to read this with an accountability partner.

7. Commit to be the spiritual leader in your marriage. Start small: read the Bible and pray together. Other options include: going through a devotional together daily and discussing it, reading or listening to a book on Christian marriage together, going through a biblical study, or serving together at church (see Rule TEN). Do *something.*

---

18 Brother Lawrence and Frank Laubach. Practicing His Presence (Jacksonville, FL: The SeedSowers, 1973).

19 Nehemiah 2:4b.

20 Psalm 139:1-18.

21 1 Peter 5:7.

22 Brother Lawrence and Frank Laubach. *Practicing His Presence* (Jacksonville, FL: The SeedSowers, 1973).

"Eat the elephant a bite at a time." Doing something is better than nothing at all – it is difficult to make a mistake here. Worst case you will fall forward. If your wife is not a believer, reflect Christ and His love in your relationship. Ask your brothers how to best do this (Proverbs 11:14).

RULE TWO:

BEFRIEND YOUR WIFE

"It is not good that the man should be alone."
Genesis 2:18

I must admit that BEFRIENDING your wife was not part of the original set of the *Guys Rules*. Not because it isn't important, quite the contrary, it is critical to any successful marriage. However, since this was a given in our marriage I just overlooked it...maybe even took it for granted. It wasn't until I was listening to Mark and Grace Driscoll's book, *Real Marriage: The Truth about Sex, Friendship and Life Together*[23], that I realized I had skipped this important foundational principle. Their book has an entire chapter dedicated to this topic.

In our home we have a sign on the wall that reads, "Happiness is being married to your best friend." This is so true! When your marriage is built upon a foundation of friendship coupled with a joint Christ centered relationship, everything else just seems to come easier; it softens the edges of the hard times, trials, and tribulations. Maintaining this friendship provides an essential foundation and glue to hold the relationship together;

---

23 Mark Driscoll and Grace Driscoll, *Real Marriage: The Truth about Sex, Friendship and Life Together* (Nashville, TN: Thomas Nelson, 2012).

then when trials come...As Ecclesiastes 4:9-10 states, "Two are better than one, because they have a good reward for their toil. For if they fall, one will lift up his fellow. But woe to him who is alone when he falls and has not another to lift him up!" I agree with Mark Driscoll when he says, "Perhaps the key is to always be working on the friendship, because in the end the rest of marriage seems to come together more easily and happily when you are working on it with your friend."[24]

From the beginning, God declared that "it was not good for man to be alone."[25] Think about it, the first thing that was NOT good in all of Creation was that man was alone. Jules Verne said, "Solitude, isolation, are painful things and beyond human endurance." To respond to this, God created a companion (a.k.a. a friend) for the man. Sadly, many a man has rejected what God has designed as ideal...that is maintaining a good companionship or friendship with one's spouse.

"This is my beloved and this is my friend."
Song of Solomon 5:16.

Is your wife your beloved AND friend? Too often the answer to this question is, "Yes and no." A husband would love his wife to the point of dying for her, but spending a few moments having a face-to-face conversation with her...well that is out of the question. Long lasting, meaningful marriages consist of two people committed to being each other's best friend.

---

24 Ibid., 27.
25 Genesis 2:18.

So, what is a good friend? The definition obviously varies from person to person. However, the following are generally accepted, though not all-inclusive, characteristics of a good friend: trustworthy, kind, honest, dependable, helpful, respectful, encouraging and can-do, loyal, empathetic, non-judgmental, generous, open, steadfast, concerned for each other's well-being, protective, caring, nurturing and edifying, a great listener, supportive, and enjoyable or fun to be around. Note how similar this list is to how Paul defined love in 1 Corinthians 13:4-8a. Also consider, for any of these characteristics to be true of a friend, they require action—they must be lived out.

> **"Happiness is being married to your best friend."**
> When your marriage is built upon a foundation of friendship coupled with a joint, Christ-centered relationship, everything else just seems to come easier; it softens the edges of the hard times, trials, and tribulations.

Do you prefer your wife's companionship over others? Has your marriage relationship become merely a heartless business relationship? I am sure it wasn't that way in the beginning. Unfortunately, many marriages "drift apart" because the couple has ceased to be friends. Spouses get caught up with the "cares of the world" (c.f. Matthew 13:22), putting children, career, paying the bills, keeping up with the Jones', or even ministry above their friendship. All these things are important; however, they should never be placed above your marriage.

Wendy, my wife, and I have made it a priority to spend time together. Furthermore, we enjoy it. However, this doesn't just happen, we put effort out to do so. However, on the surface, we really don't have much in common. She loves sitting in the hot sun while I like to be active outside in cold weather. She likes team activities, while I prefer solo activities like mountain biking and surfing. I like science fiction and fantasy...well, she just doesn't get it. Considering this, to have a great friendship or companionship it takes purpose and planning. As O. Henry said, "No friendship is an accident." Therefore, to have a successful marriage, you must make it your goal to have your wife not only be your friend, but to be your best friend.

It is interesting, when a man and a woman are courting they celebrate the differences between each other; somehow, after marriage, these differences become excuses and barriers to enjoying one another. It just doesn't have to be this way, you can be the one that causes renewal in your friendship. I understand this doesn't come naturally, especially because you probably have completely different interests. To start, it will help to understand that guy friends generally do things together, side by side, while women generally enjoy activities which require more face to face communication. When you were courting your wife, you made the effort to do this face to face communication; you must continue do it or start doing it again. This is a selfless act you can give to your wife. Many friends are takers and never give; they often suck the life out of you. After spending time with them you are not energized or stronger, but emotionally drained…are you that friend to your wife? Ultimately, if you want a better marriage, be the friend your wife would want to be with.

GOING THE EXTRA MILE

1. Scripture:
    a. Friendship: Psalm 133:1; Proverbs 8:24, 17:17; 27:9; John 15:12-15.
    b. Friendly Actions: Job 2:11; Proverbs 17:9, 27:5-6, 17, 1 Corinthians 13:4-8a, Colossians 3:12-14, Galatians 6:2; Philippians 2:4.

2. What is the state of the union of your friendship with your wife? What do you think she would she say? What areas are you most concerned about? Consider the implications of these answers? What one thing would you do first to get your friendship pointed in the right direction? Commit to make this change.

3. Ask your wife what you could do to grow your friendship. Develop a plan to address these deficiencies.

4. Do you enjoy being with other friends more than you do with your wife? Do you put more effort out to spend time with other friends more than you do with your wife? Is your wife your best friend? If your answer is "no" to any of these, write down why you think this is the case and then put a plan in place to change it.

5. Proverbs 27:5-6 says, "Better is open rebuke than hidden love. Faithful are the wounds of a friend; profuse are the kisses of an enemy." Consider this principle in your marriage. Do you have the friendship that is strong enough that you and your wife can discuss the bad news about each other's flaws in a constructive manner? Can you and your wife take the bad news without being defensive? Do you only give the good news, which implied by the passage is what an enemy would do? What could you do to have a relationship like this with your wife? One thing I always encourage people to do when receiving feedback, is to only listen and ask clarifying questions…no explanations, excuses and definitely no defensiveness. It only takes of doing the latter to shut down the benefit of future feedback. Remember, "faithful are the wounds of a friend."

6. Picture your marriage a few decades from now – the kids are gone, and you are retired. There are no more of life's distractions and it is just you and your wife. What does your day to day life with your wife look like? Does your wife wish you would go back to work? Too often retirement plans only deal with financial viability, what about your companionship plans? Discuss this with your spouse. Make a commitment to develop your long-term friendship plans.

WORK ON YOUR 10%... LET GOD DEAL WITH THE REST

First take the log out of your own eye,
and then you will see clearly to
take the speck out of your brother's eye.
Matthew 7:5b

It is human nature for people to feel like others are the bigger part of any relationship problem. At the same time, most would admit that they are at least part of the problem...even if it is *only* 10%. Marriages are not any different. You think your spouse is the bigger part of the problem, and she probably feels the same way about you. That being said, does it really matter who is more at fault? After you figure out who is responsible for their appropriate allocation of the blame, you still have to work on your part and she must work on her part. Ultimately, each of you own 100% of your own personal sanctification through abiding in the Lord.

Too often we are so consumed by the wrong – or perceived wrong – that our wife has done to us that we cannot focus on anything else, much less our own sanctification. One author said, "Anytime we think the problem is 'out there,' that thought is the problem."[26] Bitterness is consuming. It eats at your soul, it destroys your joy, and impacts all aspects of your life. A good principle for husbands to put into practice is found in Colossians 3:12-15:

> Put on then, as God's chosen ones, holy and beloved, compassionate hearts, kindness, humility, meekness, and patience, bearing with one another and, if one has a complaint against another, forgiving each other; as the Lord has forgiven you, so you also must forgive. And above all these put on love, which binds everything together in perfect harmony. And let the peace of Christ rule in your hearts, to which indeed you were called in one body. And be thankful.

As the passage above says, even if you have a complaint against your wife, you must forgive her, just as Christ also forgave you. You might ask, "What if she never apologized or asked for forgiveness for what she did to me?" Well, have you asked the Lord to forgive every sin you have committed? Even when praying the Lord's Prayer, we ask Him to forgive our debts, just as we forgive others.[27] It is interesting to note, the Amplified Version adds for clarification, "[letting go of both the wrong and the resentment]."

---

26 Stephen R. Covey, *The 7 Habits of Highly Effective People* (New York, NY: Fireside, 1989), 89.
27 Matthew 6:12.

> **"Everyone thinks of changing the world, but no one thinks of changing himself."**
> *Leo Tolstoy*
>
> The biggest waste of effort in a marriage is trying to change your spouse. It is *your* job to change *you*. NOT to change your wife..that is God's job. We serve a BIG God; He created the world, you trust Him to save you and take your sins away, you can at least trust Him to work in your wife's life. A husband's job is to trust and rest in Him. As Martin Luther said, "Pray, and let God worry."

Forgiveness, however, is freeing.[28] I like Richard Walters' definition of forgiving: "Forgiving is giving up all claims on the one who has hurt you and letting go of the emotional consequences of the hurt." It does not mean, "forgive and forget" – that is irresponsible. There are always consequences for our actions.[29] Obviously, it would not be wise to "forget" that a kleptomaniac has a problem with taking things. However, after they stole from you, you can forgive them and let go of bitterness. This is 100% your responsibility, even if it has happened four hundred and ninety times[30]. Furthermore, the Bible tells us that we are not to keep a record of wrongs or to be resentful.[31]

Ultimately, your duty is to trust the Lord to have His way with your wife. You trusted Him to save you

---

28 My brother has a great illustration on forgiveness. See Appendix F.

29 1 Kings 9:4; 11:4-5.

30 Matthew 18:21b-22. "Lord, how often will my brother sin against me, and I forgive him? As many as seven times?" Jesus said to him, "I do not say to you seven times, but seventy-seven times."

31 1 Corinthians 13:5.

and take your sins away, you can at least trust Him to work in your wife's life. You cannot control her; you must let God change her heart. *Even* if you are only 10% of the problem, you must own 100% of your part, then pray for your wife and ask God to deal with her heart, *whether* she changes or not. As much as you think you are suffering, are you really? Think of all the people in history that survived persecution, starvation, and the sword, and did so with joy by abiding in the Lord. I think you can survive a little "light and momentary affliction"[32] in your life with the Lord's help.

In relation to this attitude of owning your part, Stephen Covey says,

> If I have a problem in my marriage, what do I really gain by continually confessing my wife's sins? By saying I'm not responsible, I make myself a powerless victim; I immobilize myself in a negative situation. I also diminish my ability to influence her – my nagging, accusing, critical attitude only makes her feel validated in her own weakness. My criticism is worse than the conduct I want to correct. My ability to positively impact the situation withers and dies.
>
> If I really want to improve my situation, I can work on the one thing over which I have control – myself. I can stop trying to shape up my wife and work on my own weaknesses. I can focus on being

---

32 2 Corinthians 4:16-18.

a great marriage partner, a source of unconditional love and support. Hopefully, my wife will...respond in kind. But whether she does or doesn't, the most positive way I can influence my situation is to work on myself and my *being*.[33]

Ultimately, you must own your own vertical relationship while praying for God to work in your spouse's life. Besides, if your wife is a believer, she will welcome the prayer. Put this principle into practice: you own your part and give the rest to God – this applies to all aspects of your marriage.

For example, ever since I was nineteen years old I felt the Lord's calling to be a missionary. I had always said, "Being a missionary is a *when,* not an *if.*" Wendy understood this when she married me. Fast forward a few years, when I was in my late thirties, God had convinced me that the time had arrived. I took this revelation to my wife and she said, "God has not told me that yet." However, she asked for prayer in the matter. By this time in my life, I had learned that if she ever thought God was not in any of my decisions, it was all my fault...and it could be painful. However, the opposite was also true. So, I went to God and said, "If You want us to be missionaries in Africa, then work on Wendy's heart to convince her this is Your will." About a year later, she received her confirmation, and another year after that we were in Africa. I tell you,

---

33 Covey, *The 7 Habits of Highly Effective People*, 90.

I was so thankful I waited on God to change her heart. We were not on the ground a month before Wendy was hit with major culture shock. However, she *never* blamed me for her problem; she knew it was a vertical problem.

"Women wait on boys…Men wait on Women."

Too often wives will treat their husband like boys…because, well, they will act like boys. If you don't like being treated like a boy and want to be treated with respect, then do your part and be the person you want to be treated like. Stop acting like a good boy and act like a good man. Work on your part. One place to start is to make it your goal to be waiting on her…never let her be the one herding you out of the house. Country singer Brad Paisley got this right in his song, *Waiting on a Woman*, saying, "She'll take her time 'cause you don't mind, waitin' on a woman." Being a good man is about attending to the little things…cleaning up after yourself and not leaving a trail. Every Boy Scout knows that they should "leave no trace" in the woods. How much more should the husband leave no trace in his house…well, her house?

Hopefully, you get the point. Your job, then, is to work on your sanctification with God and pray for your wife that she will do the same. I always tell people, "work on your 10%." It acknowledges that they might not be the biggest part of the problem, or the most at fault, but through prayer and actions on their part they can love and influence the situation for better and the glory of God. Remember prayer does change things.[34] Furthermore,

---

34 Proverbs 15:29; James 5:16; 1 Peter 3:12.

let go of any bitterness; God is bigger – and the joy He provides is fuller – than any suffering or wrongs you may endure in this life.

GOING THE EXTRA MILE

1. Scripture:
    a. Bitterness: Romans 3:14; Ephesians 4:31-32; Hebrews 12:15.
    b. Forgiveness: Matthew 6:14-15; Luke 17:3-4; Mark 11:25.

2. Think about the definition for forgiveness provided in this section. What claims do you have on your spouse for hurting you? Commit to let go of the emotional hurt and give it to the Lord.

3. Think about all the time you have wasted focusing on your spouse's faults. Buddy Hackett said, "Don't carry a grudge; while you're carrying a grudge, the other guy's out dancing." I can tell you, I have wasted the equivalent of days, or even months, confessing my wife's sins. In the end, you cannot control your wife, so consequently you cannot do anything about it – only God can. Do you have issues with your wife that you have not let go of? You might be fine now, but when she does offend you, does it consume you? Commit to give these things to the Lord. Then think about what you can SPECIFICALLY do differently to make this situation better. What part do you own? What can you do to address this part?

4. Stephen Covey said, "If you ever wrap your emotional life around the weaknesses of another person you have empowered those

weaknesses to control you."[35] This is so true! Early in my marriage, I empowered my wife to control how I felt about...well, everything. If she was in a bad mood, or said something, or did something "not so nice," I *chose* to let it control my emotional life and chose to give up my joy along with it. I am not saying I am perfect at this now but realizing that it is not her fault how I *choose* to feel has helped my spiritual walk, and our marriage, significantly. Think about how you let your wife's weaknesses control your emotional life. Is your joy dependent on how well your wife treats you? What might you do to change how you respond, internally and externally, to her? Please understand, you have the freedom in Christ to choose your response in any given situation. Furthermore, the Lord is there to help you do this. How could you support your wife and respond differently in these times of "weaknesses"? See Appendix E on dealing with anger. Even if she does not return the love, respect, and support you give her in kind, remember, our peace is found in Him. Keep in mind 1 Peter 3:14-18:

> But even if you should suffer for righteousness' sake, you will be blessed. Have no fear of them, nor be troubled, but in your hearts honor Christ the Lord as holy, always being prepared to make a defense to anyone who asks you for a reason for the hope that is in you; yet do it with gentleness and respect, having a good conscience, so that, when you are slandered, those who revile your good behavior in Christ may be put to shame. For it is better to suffer for doing good,

---

35   Covey, *The 7 Habits of Highly Effective People.*

if that should be God's will, than for doing evil. For Christ also suffered once for sins, the righteous for the unrighteous, that he might bring us to God, being put to death in the flesh but made alive in the spirit.

RULE FOUR:

BE THE CHIEF SERVANT

Whoever would be great among you must be your servant, and whoever would be first among you must be slave of all.
Mark 10:43b-44

Many men think and act as though being the husband makes them the supreme commander. After all, 1 Peter 3:6 says your wife must obey your every word and call you "lord," as Sarah did to Abraham. This is one perspective…and very one sided; it is certainly not a holistic biblical perspective. Ephesians 5:25-33a, written directly to husbands, says,

> Husbands, love your wives, as Christ loved the church and gave [H]imself up for her, that he might sanctify her, having cleansed her by the washing of water with the [W]ord, so that he might present the church to himself in splendor, without spot or wrinkle or any such thing, that she might be holy and without blemish. In the same way husbands should love their wives as their own bodies. He who loves his wife loves himself. For no one ever hated his own flesh, but nourishes and cherishes it, just as Christ does the church, because we are members of his body. "Therefore a man shall leave his father and

mother and hold fast to his wife, and the two shall become one flesh." This mystery is profound, and I am saying that it refers to Christ and the church. However, let each one of you love his wife as himself.

"Ours is not to reason why, but to do and die."
Paraphrase of Alfred Lord Tennyson.

I have discovered in my marriage, whether I knew the reason why, whether I agreed or not, I ended up doing what my wife wanted. Asking why is often irrelevant and ends up being a waste of effort. Plus, she can get flustered because she had to take time to explain something. If there is not a legal, moral, or biblical issue, more often than not, I find it is just easier to do it. Often the best response is, "Yes, Dear."

First, men are not instructed to "rule" their wives, but to *love* them "as Christ loved the church and gave [H]imself up for her." Four times in this passage Paul used the word "love," which is the *agape,* unconditional type of love. He likely told us four times because men generally have to have things repeated multiple times before it sinks in and we comprehend it. Furthermore, the husband is to nourish his wife and cherish her. In our role as the "head of the wife" (Ephesians 5:23), we are to love, nourish, and cherish our wives. The question we have to ask ourselves as husbands is, "Are we reflecting the love of Christ to our wives as He does for the church?" Think about it. We are called to be a model of the same love that Christ has for us. That is not easy!

Second, Jesus compares worldly leadership to His leadership in Mark 10:42-45:

> And Jesus called them to [H]im and said to them, "You know that those who are considered rulers of the Gentiles lord it over them, and their great ones exercise authority over them. But it shall not be so among you. But whoever would be great among you must be your servant, and whoever would be first among you must be slave of all. For even the Son of Man came not to be served but to serve, and to give [H]is life as a ransom for many."

Jesus clearly calls leaders to be servants. Thus, He is calling husbands not to be lords of the family but to be the servant leader of the household. Thus, the biblical attitude of the husband must be that of *Chief Servant* of the home.

If it is important to her, make it important to you.

It is often cited that women average speaking twenty thousand words per day. They will want to do this with someone who cares and shows interest. If you are not this person, she will often find someone else who will. Many a marriage has broken up "because we don't communicate." As Susan Scott said in her book, *Fierce Conversations*, "If it's important to that person, then it's important. So go there." Listening is part of the service and honor due to your wife; focus on hearing what her cares and concerns are – don't be a critic or look to fix things. Be her special ear.

My favorite book on leadership is *The Servant* by James C. Hunter.[36] It is a fictional story about true leadership; which manifests itself as servant leadership. The premise of the book is this:

Leadership is about influence. → Who has influenced more people in the history of the world...? Jesus. → What did He teach?

In his book, Hunter says, "The role of leadership is to serve, that is, to identify and meet legitimate needs. In the process of meeting needs, we often will be called to make sacrifices for those we serve."[37] This is the job of the husband: to identify the *needs,* not *wants,* of his wife and then the family. Furthermore, Hunter discusses that this takes influence, and there are two ways to do this. First is the common method of using *power*, and the second is with *authority*. Using *power*, is essentially giving someone no other option to bend to your will through force, threats, or coercion. This might work occasionally but when used often it destroys the relationship. Hunter quotes Margaret Thatcher, "Being in power is like being a lady. If you have to remind people that you are, you aren't."[38] Authority, on the other hand, is getting people to *willingly* do what you want them to do because of your personal influence...it is more about character.[39]

---

36 Hunter, *The Servant*.
37 Ibid., 85.
38 Ibid., 15.
39 Ibid., 30.

Every time you *use* power to influence your wife (if you can even get away with it) or your kids, you must ask yourself if there was a way you could have handled this better to prevent this use of power. Understand that there are times when power is completely needed, like if your wife is about to put herself or others in danger or do a unilateral act that would seriously impact your finances. However, every time you use power, ask yourself how you might have handled the situation differently, so you will not need to influence her in this manner in the future. Think about it, a real servant would never use power because he would understand he did not have the authority to do so. In the end, as much as it depends on you, follow Jesus' example and be the leader by being the Chief Servant.

GOING THE EXTRA MILE

1. Scripture:
   a. Jesus the servant: Matthew 20:28; Mark 9:33-35; 10:45; John 13:12-15; Philippians 2:3-8.
   b. Be a servant: Luke 22:26; Acts 20:35; 1 Peter 5:1-5.

2. Think about the legitimate needs of your wife – beyond food, clothing, and a house. In many ways, it is easier for us husbands to take a bullet for our wives than it would be to try to figure out what their needs are and then meet them. After all, once you figure it out, it will probably change (See Appendix B). No matter how difficult this might be, it does not get us off the hook. Make the effort to try to figure out her needs. There are two books that I have

found helpful: *For Men Only*[40], by Shaunti and Jeff Feldhahn, and *If Only He Knew*[41], by Gary Smalley. Make a list of three key legitimate needs of your wife and how you will specifically meet these.

3.   Have you used power in your relationship with your wife? How could you have avoided this? Think of the definition of authority. How could you develop more authority in your relationship with your wife?

4.   Stephen Covey quotes an essay by E.M. Gray entitled, "The Denominator of Success,"

> "[E.M. Gray] deals with the author's life long search for the one denominator that all successful people share. He found it wasn't hard work, good luck, or astute human relations, though those are all important." One factor seemed to transcend all the rest…the essence of Habit 3—putting first things first. "The successful person has the habit of doing the things failures don't like to do…They don't like doing them either necessarily. But their disliking is subordinated to the strength of their purpose."[42]

I have found this to be true in marriage too. In short, if you want to have success in life, especially in marriage, you will have to do

---

40   Shaunti Feldhahn, and Jeff Feldhahn. *For Men Only* (Atlanta, GA: Random House, 2006).

41   Gary Smalley. *If Only He Knew* (Grand Rapids: Zondervan, 2012).

42   Covey, *The 7 Habits of Highly Effective People, 148-149.*

things you do not want to do. What are some of those things that you do not want to do, but if you started doing them would make your marriage more successful?

5. Being a servant leader in your marriage is often like herding or shepherding cats. Cats are independent and strong willed. Yes, you can make a cat do something, but it takes brute force and has lasting negative consequences to that relationship. Our wives are like cats that we are called to lead. We must encourage them, coax them, and love them unconditionally to lead them. Considering this reality, how might you better shepherd your wife?

LOVE IS A VERB

Husbands, love your wives [with an affectionate, sympathetic, selfless love that always seeks the best for them] and do not be embittered or resentful toward them [because of the responsibilities of marriage].

Colossians 3:19 (AMP)

Biblical love is NOT a feeling, it is a verb. Husbands are called to love their wives in actions and deeds. The go-to passage to describe Christian love is found in 1 Corinthians 13:1-8a. Many of you had these verses read in your wedding. Notice that this passage is about what you *do* and not your feelings – it is unconditional *agape* love.

Following is a personal marriage covenant of love based upon these verses as found in the Amplified Bible, which we should all aspire daily to put into practice:

Marriage Covenant of Love:

I will…

- be patient and kind.

- never act envious.

- not be boastful or vainglorious—not display myself haughtily.

- not act conceited, arrogant, or inflated with pride.

- not behave rudely, act unmannerly, or act unbecomingly.

- not insist on my own rights or own way—not be self-seeking.

- not be touchy, fretful, or resentful.

- keep no account or record of a wrong done to me.

- not rejoice at injustice or immoral behavior, but I will rejoice when right and truth prevail.

- suffer patiently under any circumstances and everything that comes.

- edify and constructively build up my wife (whether present or not).

- be ever ready to believe the best in my spouse.

- endure everything without weakening.

- maintain these principles because I know they will never fail, fade out, become obsolete, or come to an end.

Again, this is all about a love that is a verb. It has been said, "love is as love does." We might have the best intentions, but if our actions do not align with them then it means nothing. Our actions have to align with our intentions. This is why Jesus can say, "Love your enemies."[43]

---

43   Matthew 5:44; Luke 6:27, 35.

Now let us be clear, your wife is NOT your enemy, but the point is, we are not called to *feel* love towards our enemies, but to *act* in love towards our enemies. If we can practice love to our enemies, how great should that love be for our wives? James Hunter says, "You cannot always control how you are going to feel about another person [your wife] but you can control [or choose] how you are going to behave toward that person [your wife.]"[44] Thus, as Gary Smalley says, "love is a decision;" he understood that love is a choice of action.

Another passage which pertains to how believers should act in general, which applies directly toward how we should behave in marriage, is Romans 12:9-21. Here are some of the highlights:

- Let love [the verb] be genuine.

- Abhor what is evil; hold fast to what is good.

- Outdo one another in showing honor.

- Be patient in tribulation.

- Be constant in prayer.

- Bless those who persecute you; bless and do not curse them.

- Rejoice with those who rejoice, weep with those who weep.

- Live in harmony with one another.

---

44 Hunter, *The Servant*, 98.

- Do not be haughty; never be wise in your own sight.

- Repay no one evil for evil but give thought to do what is honorable in the sight of all.

- If possible, so far as it depends on you, live peaceably with all.

- Beloved, never avenge yourselves.

- Do not be overcome by evil but overcome evil with good.

Not to be repetitive, but we are men and need to have things repeated to us – the bullets above are choices in behavior. One that really hits home with me is "Outdo one another in showing honor." Striving to do a better job of honoring her than she does for you could be the only sanctioned competition in marriage.

Hit the Pause Button.

When your wife is talking to you while you are watching TV, just hit the pause button. The game or show isn't going anywhere. Let her know by your actions that she is more important than what is on TV…because she is. Also, if your wife is trying to communicate with you but you are distracted by something and unable to focus, ask her to pause a second "because you want to give her your undivided attention," then address the distraction so you can truly listen to her. For example, in our house the TV is often on for "background" noise. I ask her to "hold that thought" while I pause the TV, then I can give her that attention she deserves.

Considering the last few bullets above, not that your wife is evil or your enemy, but that your job is always to overcome frustration and adversity with good, never avenging yourself or paying her back for an offense done against you. We are to "overlook an offense," as Proverbs 17:9 says. Abraham Lincoln said, "Folks are usually about as happy as they make their minds up to be." The same holds for your marriage.

There is a book called *Man's Search for Meaning,* written by a Jewish psychologist named Victor Frankl who survived the German concentration camps during World War II. In this book, he shares his experiences, focusing more on people's responses to the cruelty they endured than what was done to them. When he finishes his story, he analyses the experience; obviously, he is uniquely qualified to discuss suffering and our response to it. He discovered:

> We who lived in concentration camps can remember the men who walked through the huts comforting others, giving away their last piece of bread. They may have been few in number but they offer sufficient proof that everything can be taken from a man but one thing: the last of the human freedoms—to choose one's attitude in any given set of circumstances, to choose one's own way...in the final analysis it becomes clear that the sort of person the prisoner became was a result of an inner decision, and not the result of camp influences alone.[45]

---

45   Victor E. Frankl, *Man's Search for Meaning* (New York, NY: Simon & Schuster, 1984), 75.

Remember that the Little Things are the BIG Things.

Let her know regularly and in diverse ways that you love her and are thinking about her. Leave notes, texts, e-mails, etc. saying you love her, she is beautiful, or you miss her. Be creative and do it WEEKLY. Call her during the middle of the day and let her know that you are thinking of her. She might be busy and not want to talk long, but she will appreciate it. Flowers or something sweet on occasion, when it is NOT a special day, is important. Bruce Barton said, "Sometimes when I consider what tremendous consequences come from little things...I am tempted to think... there are no little things." Just recently, I put some Post-its on my wife's car windshield with hearts and an, "I Love U." Even after twenty-nine years of marriage, this makes her feel special. Furthermore, remember that there are five big days in a year: Christmas, Valentine's Day, Mother's Day, your anniversary, and her birthday. If she says they are not a big deal, or you don't have to do anything...it is a LIE! It's a trap! Don't ever believe it. For some reason women regularly do this. I think it has to do with wanting to be pragmatic, but when it comes down to it, they are really hoping you won't be able to control yourself because you love them so much.

Early in my marriage, I would regularly say, "My wife can play me like a piano." I was her plaything as I had given the control of my emotional state to her. I took no ownership of my choices and responses. However, when I considered that I have never been through anything closely as horrible as what Dr. Frankl went through, I realized I had no excuse – I am therefore obligated to own how I respond and act in all I do. Commenting on Frankl, Stephen Covey said, "Between stimulus and response is our greatest power – the freedom to choose."[46] That is to choose how we respond to what life brings us. I discovered I must own both my vertical and horizontal relationships, and consequently, I am responsible and able to choose to love my wife and act lovingly in all circumstances through Christ.

GOING THE EXTRA MILE

1. Scripture:
    a. Love is willing to die, or even more: John 15:13; Romans 5:7-8; Ephesians 5:2.
    b. Accept her: Romans 14:1-15:7.

2. I have heard husbands say they love their wives enough to die for them, and I truly believe they would. That is easy and tangible... it is black and white. However, dealing with the gray areas of a relationship with a woman is another thing. Loving them enough to sacrifice and listen to them and try to understand them is a cross difficult to bear. What kinds of things are difficult for you to bear in your relationship? What could you do differently to really demonstrate your love to your spouse? Yes, this might be more difficult than dying for her. Commit to do this and tell a friend to hold you accountable to do it.

3. The *New Living Translation* of Romans 15:7 says, "Therefore, accept each other just as Christ has accepted you so that God will be given

---

46 Covey, *The 7 Habits of Highly Effective People*, 70.

glory." How could you demonstrate the love that Christ has for us by accepting your wife in the way Christ has accepted you?

4. Do a word study on all the attributes, or verbs if you will, that describe love in 1 Corinthians 13:4-7. Where do you have opportunity to apply these in your marriage? Put an action plan together to address these.

RULE SIX:

LEAVE AND CLEAVE

Therefore a man shall leave his father and his mother and hold fast [cleave] to his wife, and they shall become one flesh.
Genesis 2:24

After Creation, the first thing God addresses is the relationship of the man and the woman – marriage. He says that the husband is supposed to leave his parents and cleave to his wife. There are two very important parts to this very basic instruction: to leave and to cleave.

The first part of this proclamation is that we are supposed to leave our parents. You are a new family unit and your wife is now the number one human in your life. Not your parents, or your extended family, and not your children. The husband-wife relationship is designed to be permanent, as long as you both shall live. The parent-child relationship is temporary, that is true for your relationship with your parents and with your children. God put a husband and his wife in the garden, not a parent and a child.[47] Therefore, you need to act accordingly. There will be times in your marriage when you will have to make decisions which give precedence to your marriage over your birth family unit's desires.

---

47   Jay E. Adams, *Christian Living in the Home* (Phillipsburg, NJ: P&R, 1972), 52.

You will learn that it will cause you difficulty in your marriage when you regularly run to your parents or siblings whenever you are having issues with your wife. What often happens in this scenario is the family only seems to hear about the negative issues and problems in the relationship. Because this is all they hear, they assume it is all bad – they think your wife is a horrible person who "always" makes you upset. Since running to another woman for advice is most definitely unwise, I would suggest you find a mentor and speak with him when you have marriage issues.

In his book *Strengthening Your Marriage*, Wayne Mack lists the following four principles that must be radically changed in your relationship with your parents:[48]

1. It means that you establish an adult relationship with them.

2. It means that you must be more concerned about your mate's ideas, opinions, and practices than those of your parents.

3. It means that you must not be slavishly dependent on your parents for affection, approval, assistance, and counsel.

---

48   Wayne A. Mack, *Strengthening Your Marriage* (Phillipsburg, NJ: P&R, 1977), 2.

4. It means that you must eliminate any bad
    attitudes towards your parents, or you
    will be tied emotionally to them regard-
    less of how far you move from them.

The second principle in this verse is that you must
cleave to your wife. She is now the number one woman
in your life. She is the queen and must be treated as
such. There can be no more girlfriends – that is, no
more friendly relationships with women that are private
or personal. Many say this is old fashioned, but I have
learned the hard way that this is the only safe way. Avoid
being alone with women and having conversations deeper
than the weather unless your wife is present. Earlier in
my marriage, I strived to be a nice guy and was regularly
empathetic and attentive to women, and consequently,
not once but twice, I had women "offer" themselves to
me. Because of these experiences, I learned I needed to
flee any "friendly" situations with the opposite sex. This is
also honoring to our wives.

On another occasion, when I was new to Africa, the
daughter of one of my employees had tuberculosis (TB).
If you do not know about TB, it is a nasty disease. This
young woman went from 130 pounds down to about 70
pounds until she was literally skin and bones. The treatment lasts over six months, and if you miss one day of
treatment then you must start over. She was literally at
death's door. For some reason, I felt responsible to help
her, as no one else seemed to step up. I poured myself

into taking care of her needs. I am convinced, and others are too, that if I had not taken this personal responsibility then she would have died. She is now healthy, and even got married recently.

In spite of the good that came to this girl, I am ashamed that I never engaged my wife in this "ministry." In fact, I not only didn't engage Wendy, I neglected her. As the old saying goes, "The ends cannot justify the means." During this time, my wife definitely did not feel like the queen. In fact, I had essentially abandoned her in a foreign land. 1 Timothy 5:8 exhorts us not to neglect our household or we are worse than unbelievers (See Rule EIGHT). Obviously, this would apply to our wives more than to anyone else – ouch! To make a long story short, I repented publicly to our friends, church, and family. Unfortunately, it is quite common for men in ministry to neglect their marriage like I did. This is *not* biblical....and *not* cleaving to or meeting the needs of your wife.

Cleaving is more than being attracted to your wife, though this is an important and foundational biblical principle of marriage. Some of the favorite verses of us married men are Proverbs 5:18-19[49], 1 Corinthians 7:2-5[50], and

---

49 Proverbs 5:18-19. "Let your fountain be blessed, and rejoice in the wife of your youth, a lovely deer, a graceful doe. Let her breasts fill you at all times with delight; be intoxicated always in her love."

50 1 Corinthians 7:2-5. "But because of the temptation to sexual immorality, each man should have his own wife and each woman her own husband. The husband should give to his wife her conjugal rights, and likewise the wife to her husband. For the wife does not have authority over her own body, but the husband does. Likewise the husband does not have authority over his own body, but the wife does. Do not deprive one another, except perhaps by agreement for a limited time, that you may devote yourselves to prayer; but then come together again, so that Satan may not tempt you because of your lack of self-control."

Hebrews 13:4[51]. Not to make light of them as they certainly are a critical part of cleaving to your wife; you should have eyes and thoughts for her only. Matthew 5:28b tells us, "[E]veryone who looks at a woman with lustful intent has already committed adultery with her in his heart." Thus, you are not only welcome to desire your wife, but it is encouraged.

That being said, cleaving is deeper than sexual attraction. Do you make time for your wife? When you are together, are you actually present...that is, are you more than just physically there? Are you on your phone or watching sports on TV? You might even be doing household chores. All these can send the message to your wife that other things are more important than her...that she is not the most important person in your life (a.k.a. the queen).

Children also compete for attention. Jay Adams says in his book *Christian Living in the Home* that:

> Parents who have built their lives around their children frequently end up in our counseling center around the time the last child is leaving home. Because they have lived for their children all these years, their talk, their interests, their schedules, indeed, their whole life structure has been built around the children.[52]

---

51 Hebrews 13:4. "Let marriage be held in honor among all, and let the marriage bed be undefiled, for God will judge the sexually immoral and adulterous."

52 Adams, *Christian Living in the Home*, 52.

Therefore, you need to make the effort to be mentally present when you spend time with your wife. Susan Scott says, "Be here, be prepared to be nowhere else."[53] One way to do this is to date your wife; it is a novel idea, you should try it! I think this is important enough that I have a friend in Africa who I ask every month over Skype, "Have you had your three dates with your wife this month?" You can be creative; dates do not all have to cost money. You can go on a bike ride together, watch a movie at home when the kids go down, or get up early and eat breakfast together before the kids wake up. Early in our marriage we used to feed the ducks at a local pond. You also need to go on vacations together; *do not* talk yourselves out of it – regular getaways where you are alone together is important. Remember Matthew 6:21, "For where your treasure is, there your heart will be also." After the Lord, she must be first. If you value her, make the time.

Don't Complain to Momma!

Too often when there are difficulties in a marriage, husbands will *vent* to their mothers. Yes, our parents are valuable counselors when we go to them to constructively to seek advice and help, however, they are not there for us to complain to. If all Momma hears is negative, she will develop an incorrect picture of your spouse and your relationship. Don't complain or grumble against your wife; it will not help your marriage, and it is unbiblical (Philippians 2:14, James 5:9, Ephesians 4:29).

---

53   Scott, *Fierce Conversations*, 91.

Cleaving to your wife means that you recognize you are incomplete without her. I always say tongue in cheek, "God gave me a wife to ensure I am humble," but I really mean that God gave her to me to make me a better man.

One last thought: if she has "something against you," you have a responsibility "so far as it depends on you to live peaceably with all [including your wife]."[54] Even if you are at church or in ministry, Matthew 5:23-24 says, "So if you are offering your gift at the altar and there remember that your brother [or wife] has something against you, leave your gift there before the altar and go. First be reconciled to your brother [or wife], and then come and offer your gift."

G O I N G   T H E   E X T R A   M I L E

1.   Scripture:

    a.   Cleave: Deuteronomy 10:20; 11:22; 13:4,17; 28:21, 60; 30:20.

    b.   Matters of the heart and mind: Matthew 5:28;
        Job 31:1; Proverbs 6:25; 2 Samuel 11:2-4, Matthew 6:21,
        Romans 12:1-2, 2 Corinthians 10:5.

2.   Evaluate each of the four points that Wayne Mack said above regarding leaving your family. Are there any issues here in your life? What could you do better? What will you do differently?

3.   The Hebrew word translated "cleave" or "hold fast" is used 52 times in the Old Testament. Consider the verses above regarding

---

54   Romans 12:18.

cleaving; not only are we exhorted in Genesis 2:24 to "hold fast" to our wives, but the same word is used with respect to "holding fast" to the Lord. What implications are there in your marriage? What might you do differently about it?

4. Holding fast to the Lord or your wife starts in the heart. We know what happened to David when he did not cleave in his heart...he fell into sin[55], and the whole nation suffered for it. Jesus takes it further. He essentially says David committed adultery not when he looked, but after he looked and lusted. Cleaving is more than guarding your heart or avoiding bad situations. Cleaving is actively desiring your wife in your mind and heart. Are you cleaving to your wife in your heart? How could you do this better?

5. When you got married, I am sure you loved spending time with your wife...she was your best friend. Is she now? Is she the queen? Either way, what can you specifically do better in this area?

6. My brother supplied this: One year I must admit I wasn't feeling very "cleavy" or affectionate toward my wife. I was finding my mind occupied by other things, even temptations. I also noticed she was feeling it, even if I was trying to put my best face on it. It was before Valentine's Day, so I took a cue from Christmas and enacted the Twelve Days of Valentine's. Every day for twelve days I did something special. I spent about $50 on cards, candies, gift cards, etc. Nothing elaborate. I left her a card. I'd leave chocolate with a funny note. I made Lego dolls depicting the two of

---

55   2 Samuel 11-12.

us. I would leave the lyrics to a song. I would post something on Facebook or Instagram. By the time we reached Valentine's Day, my heart was fully changed back, and she felt SO incredibly spoiled. It was all such simple stuff. Just an acknowledgment and daily reminder of our love. But it makes all the difference.

UNDERSTAND YOUR WIFE:

*Likewise, husbands, live with your wives
in an understanding way, showing honor to
the woman as the weaker vessel, since they are
heirs with you of the grace of life,
so that your prayers may not be hindered.*

1 Peter 3:7

Do you want your prayers hindered? Well, Peter is saying that if we do not live with our wife in an understanding way and honor her as the weaker vessel, this is exactly what will happen. This actually makes logical sense. If we do not do these things, it is natural for our wives to feel neglected, then they get upset...and everyone knows, "If momma ain't happy, ain't nobody happy." Now this might not be completely true, but there is always a little bit of truth in these clever anecdotes. So, if your wife is upset with you, generally it will impact, if not dominate, the rest of your life. In short, the condition of our horizontal relationship with our wives naturally impacts the condition of our vertical relationship with the Lord. Therefore, grasping what Peter is communicating is important. Let us dissect this more.

It is NOT a Question.

When your wife asks you a question, like, "Do you think that would look better over there?" or "Do you think somebody should wash the car?" It is probably NOT a question but a request. I don't know why women do this – why can't they just ask? It's one of life's great mysteries – it is what it is. Therefore, keep this thought at the top of your mind: many questions she asks are actually requests. For example, just recently, my wife asked me if there was something left in an ice chest that was in the car. I said, "I don't know," and then just sat there. She said, "Well aren't you going to check?" This was a classic case of me forgetting this tip – she was asking me to go check to see if it was in the ice chest. Silly me.

Husbands are to live with their wives in an understanding way. To do this well, it requires the man to put her needs above his. The fifth habit of Stephen Covey's *The 7 Habits of Highly Effective People*, is to "Seek first to understand, then to be understood." The first thing that I tend to do when my wife is upset with me is to convince her that "I did not mean to..." In other words, I want her to understand me first. The loving thing to do would be to understand that I hurt her and then ask for forgiveness. Note, I did not say apologize or say, "I am sorry." For some reason, this is what we do in our American culture. The Bible only exhorts us to ask for forgiveness, never to apologize. Asking for forgiveness requires humility and a contrite spirit.[56]

---

56 Psalm 51:17. "The sacrifices of God are a broken spirit; a broken and contrite heart, O God, you will not despise."

Understanding her is more than listening, you must figure out what she is communicating. As much as you want the love of your life to write things in crayon, just accept that she is not capable, and therefore will not. Listen more deeply to what she is communicating. This takes effort and conscious thought. Hear more than just the words by recognizing tone and body language. She might say, "This is the worst day of my life." The typical male response is, "No it's not; remember the time...." What you just did was invalidate her feelings and communicate to her that you were not listening or understanding what she was saying. A better response might be, "It sounds like it is a difficult day. I am here for you."

Have you ever listened hard and tried to help her by suggesting a solution only to be accused of not listening? Well, generally, she does not want you to fix her problem. I know that is what we men do, we fix things. However, listening and responding with empathy is all she wants.[57] It has been said, "When a woman asks your opinion, she does not want to hear your opinion; she wants to hear her opinion in a deeper voice." Make a conscious effort to be an ear. My wife works at a club store stocking shelves, and I know everything about her job because she shares with me daily her struggles and difficulties. My daughter does the same thing, giving me her daily play-by-play recap of her day. They both

---

57   For a great video on this concept, go to YouTube and type in the search window, "It's Not About the Nail." I have shared this video in a marriage workshop and every woman agreed this was exactly how they felt...

generally only want to vent...what they are looking for is empathy, not for me to fix anything. I always say, "Because my wife cares...I care." Just listen, as Susan Scott says, "If it's important to that person [your wife], then it is important. So go there."[58]

"What she wanted yesterday, may NOT be what she wants today."

It has been said that it's a woman's prerogative to change her mind. If this is true about your wife, just go with it. It is like the wind – can you really know its direction tomorrow? If your wife wanted something one way yesterday, it may change today. This might not be a politically correct view; however, my wife admits that many women are this way. If you have a wife like this, don't fret. Don't fight it; doing so would be like fighting the ocean tides. Think positively about this – it keeps life interesting and provides you another opportunity to serve her.

Furthermore, women are generally more feelings-oriented. So we show honor to our wives by not reacting directly to what they say or feel. Often, our wives will say things with so much passion that it feels as if we are to blame or they are upset with us. Sometimes it feels like it is disrespectful, or that she is treating me as like a child. At this point, I have a decision to make, do I listen with empathy or make it about me?[59] As a general rule, whenever I have made it about me versus listening

---

58 Scott, *Fierce Conversations*, 107.

59 Gary Chapman's book, *Anger: Handling a Powerful Emotion in a Healthy Way*, is very helpful in this area. We all get angry, however, rarely do people have a plan to deal with it. Most just "wing it." It is available in audio too.

with empathy, things have gotten bad quickly. Early in our marriage, this decision would literally wreck our relationship for days. Nowadays, I usually do a good job at listening with empathy, however, occasionally I still fail. My wife said to me recently, "Most of the time you are a great listener, then you will go off and I don't know why; you blindside me." I realized that one "oops" has a significant impact on her. So being an understanding husband is about putting her first – it is another way of being the *Chief Servant*. Solomon had it right when he said, "Good sense makes one slow to anger, and it is his glory to overlook an offense."[60] When I do not take things personally or make it about me, things go great. When I practice this, it does not take long before she is smiling like nothing happened.

"If she repeats herself, it is important."

If your wife repeats something, she is communicating to you that it is important and wants this something to be addressed. Listen for these subtle repeat queues. Seek to understand why she is repeating herself. In many cases it is because she doesn't feel listened to or understood. It might be something as simple as, "I noticed you said this twice, is there something you don't feel I am doing or hearing?"

Another thing to consider as men is that we like to say, "be a man and deal with it" or "suck it up." I have three boys and I expect them to act like men and "man

---

60 Proverbs 19:11.

up." However, with my daughter I would never say that; I would listen to her vent all day. Here is a public service announcement for you men with daughters: careful that you do not treat you daughter like the queen. Your wife is the queen, your daughter is only the princess. I have made my wife jealous many a time because I have been known to give my daughter more empathy than I do to her.

Moving to the second part of this verse, we are told to show "honor to the woman as the weaker vessel." This is more than opening doors for her, though this is a great start. When we open the door for her, we are showing her honor. Yes, she is completely capable of opening the door, but when I do it for her, I honor her. My wife is a morning person, so after dinner she is generally on life support. When the kids were young, I was in charge of the process of getting them into bed. Nowadays she needs her phone by her bed at night as an alarm for work at four in the morning. I cannot tell you the number of times I have had to go downstairs and find that stupid phone because my all-but-lifeless wife forgot to bring it to bed with her. At the moment she is weakest, it is my job to be strong for her – no matter how tired I personally might feel myself. This is how we show honor to her as the weaker vessel. Consider what Paul says in Romans 15:1-2, "We who are strong have an obligation to bear with the failings of the weak, and not to please ourselves. Let each of us please his neighbor for his good, to build him up." I would think our wives are clearly our closest neighbor…that is, if she does not make you sleep in the dog house.

We are called to be servants. Who else should we serve more than our wives? Consider the attitude Jesus calls us to have:

> Will any one of you who has a servant plowing or keeping sheep say to him when he has come in from the field, "Come at once and recline at table"? Will he not rather say to him, "Prepare supper for me, and dress properly, and serve me while I eat and drink, and afterward you will eat and drink"? Does he thank the servant because he did what was commanded? So you also, when you have done all that you were commanded, say, "We are unworthy servants; we have only done what was our duty."[61]

Yes, we are "unworthy servants." This must be our attitude in all we do, especially with our wives.

I will close with this thought. The verses following 1 Peter 3:7 give a little hint on how to understand and honor our wives:

> Finally, all of you, have unity of mind, sympathy, brotherly love, a tender heart, and a humble mind. Do not repay evil for evil or reviling for reviling, but on the contrary, bless, for to this you were called, that you may obtain a blessing.[62]

---

61 Luke 17:7.
62 1 Peter 3:8-9.

GOING THE EXTRA MILE

1. Scripture:

    a. Listen: 1 Kings 3:9; Proverbs 2:2; 18:2, 13; James 1:19.

    b. Overlook an offense: Ecclesiastes 7:20-22; Proverbs 12:16; 13:3; 21:23; Romans 12:16,18.

2. Read 1 Peter 3:7-12 and break it down into its components. How would you apply this to your marriage?

3. In her book *Fierce Conversations*, Susan Scott exhorts us to "[b]e here, prepared to be nowhere else…speak and listen as if this is the most important conversation you will have with this person. It could be. Participate as if it matters. It does."[63] How could you put this principle into practice with your wife? I am distracted easily…it is an A.D.D. thing; one thing I do is turn off the TV or pause it when my wife wants to talk. We all have DVR's now anyway, you are not going to miss anything. Treat your wife like she is more important than what is on TV…because she is! Even if she always seems to wait until the most critical point in the game or movie to have a conversation.

4. Go to YouTube and type in the search window, "It's Not About the Nail." I have shared this video with married couples, and every time the women agree that they often feel this way. Do you act like the man in this video? Does your wife act like the woman? I bet you both do. What could you do differently in your conversations with your wife to make her feel more understood and edified? Practice

---

63 Scott, *Fierce Conversations*, 91.

listening with empathy while seeking to understand. At the same time, make it about her, do not make it about you, and don't give advice *unless* she specifically asks for it.

5.   If you or your wife struggle with anger, grab a copy of Gary Chapman's book *Anger: Handling a Powerful Emotion in a Healthy Way*, and read or listen to it.[64]

6.   Read the article "Listening to your Wife" in Appendix D. It is a paraphrased excerpt from a book called *Life Together* written by Dietrich Bonhoeffer. He was talking about the ministry of listening in the church. I just changed it to relate specifically to our wives.

---

64   Gary Chapman, *Anger: Handling a Powerful Emotion in a Healthy Way*, (Chicago: Northfield Publishing, 2007).

PROVIDE FOR THE NEEDS OF YOUR WIFE

But if anyone does not provide for his relatives,
and especially for members of his household,
he has denied the faith and is worse than an unbeliever.

1 Timothy 5:8

Can you believe that? If we do not provide for our households, and this would definitely include our wives, we are worse than unbelievers! Too often I know I do not take this responsibility seriously. This is more than just meeting material needs, but it starts there. Are you providing for your wife's spiritual and emotional needs? Again, we are talking about *needs,* not *wants.* As I mentioned before, it is our job to identify, and then meet, the legitimate needs of our wives. We regularly need to step back, look at the big picture, and identify the ever-changing needs of our wives.[65] And yes, what she needs today will be different tomorrow, or as I often say, "What was right yesterday, will not be right today." The sooner you realize and accept this truth, the better you will be. Do not fight it, go with it. As husbands, we are responsible for all the big

---

65 Hunter, *The Servant,* 85.

decisions and the direction of the family. Most decisions are not any more important than whether I eat an apple or a banana. If she wants a green wall or pink carpet, does it really matter that much?

Win - Win Weekends.

Before the weekend starts, you and your wife share what is the most important task you each want to accomplish. After you agree what these are, commit to each other to make it a priority. If your wife wants you to mow the lawn and go to a movie, and you want to go golfing, work to schedule these activities into the weekend plan then work everything else around these. This way you both get what you want...a win-win.

One need for our wives is for them to feel trusted. Stephen Covey says, "Trust is the highest form of human motivation."[66] If our wives feel trusted, they will strive to live up to that trust. James Hunter says, "Without trust, it is difficult, if not impossible, to maintain a good relationship. Trust is the glue that holds the relationship together."[67] Then he asks the question, "How many good relationships do you have with people you do not trust?" I bet it is not many, if any at all. Thus, trust is of critical importance.

Trust must go both ways. Security is critical to a woman's emotional needs. Obviously, Jesus needs to be our Rock, however, if we are supposed to love our wives

---

66 Covey, *The 7 Habits of Highly Effective People*, 178.
67 Hunter, *The Servant*.

as Christ loves the church,[68] then we must reflect Him by being her rock. Furthermore, trust is built on character. She will not trust you if your character is questionable. Ralph Waldo Emerson said, "What you are shouts so loudly in my ears I cannot hear what you say." Covey says, "What we are communicates far more eloquently than anything we say or do."[69] We must reflect Christ, but how?

No matter how much effort we put out, John 15:4-5 tells us that if we do not abide in Him, no matter the intent, it will be useless:

> Abide in me, and I in you. As the branch cannot bear fruit by itself, unless it abides in the vine, neither can you, unless you abide in me. I am the vine; you are the branches. Whoever abides in me and I in him, he it is that bears much fruit, for apart from me you can do nothing.

Character begins with abiding in Him. By abiding with Him, we will walk with Him and naturally display the fruit of the Spirit, "[T]he fruit of the Spirit is love, joy, peace, patience, kindness, goodness, faithfulness, gentleness, self-control; against such things there is no law."[70]

---

68 Ephesians 5:25. "Husbands, love your wives, as Christ loved the church and gave himself up for her."

69 Covey, *The 7 Habits of Highly Effective People*, p.22.

70 Galatians 5:22-23.

What woman would not want or need this? Through Him we must walk in the Spirit for our wives' sake.

Don't Argue About Feelings.

Often a woman can make strong declarative statements when her emotions have gotten the best of her. She might say, "This is the worst day ever." Now the first thing we as husbands want to do is explain that there were in fact many more worse days in her past. But then we are not hearing what she is communicating. She is just having a bad day, and it FEELS like the worst day ever. When this happens, it can feel like she is in the "What have you done for me lately?" syndrome. Last week you were the best husband in the world, and now you are the worst. Don't hear what she is *saying*, hear what she is *communicating*. This is where you have an opportunity to meet her needs and respond with empathy. Don't argue about words, don't ask for an explanation, don't get flustered, and especially don't mock it. It is NOT about you, it is about her – meet her need of empathy.

This can work the other way too. My wife just recently said, "This was the best Mother's Day ever." Now I am thinking, what about all those days I busted my butt for you taking care of the kids so you didn't have to do anything on your slave day – I mean Mother's Day? Again, it is NOT about you... just be happy for her.

The next need of a wife which a husband is responsible to meet is creating a proper environment[71] for her and children to thrive in. Similarly, in the work place, it is often amazing to me how much people will put up

---

71 Chapter Five of *The Servant*, by Hunter covers this topic in detail.

with when they are respected and trusted. However, when they do not receive respect and trust, people will often quit or seek a union for help. In marriage, wives "quit" by seeking a divorce or they will seek "help" by getting empathy and value elsewhere, which can lead to adultery. Often, employees will cite money as their issue, however, it is common knowledge that money never is the primary reason for their discontent. Likewise, in marriage, couples will cite money as an issue, however, it never is the root of the problem. Money is the catalyst for other problems; it is like gasoline on a fire. Think about all those poor, newly-married kids who live on love...they usually are living on less than those getting divorced for money issues.

Think about the farmer. He does not make the plants grow, that is God's job. He is responsible to create the best conditions for the crop to grow and thrive. Likewise, the husband has the same responsibility. The crop of a farmer needs constant attention, and so do our wives.

Most men understand the importance of preventive maintenance for their cars, especially those men who have given their car a name. If you do not perform scheduled maintenance in a timely and regular manner, the car will break down, and then you will have big problems. Plus, not doing the little things required to keep your car going demonstrates to it and everyone else that you do not care for it (Yes, cars have feelings too). Likewise, our wives react in the same manner when we do not do the little things to maintain the relationship. If we do not do our regular maintenance on our marriage, it will break down. Then you will have big problems...you will wish it *was* only your car that was broken. I always say, "My wife is not high maintenance, she just requires regular maintenance." If she is feeling neglected, I am reminded that I have failed to do my part. My wife is pretty easy. If I give her the attention to which she is rightfully due, life is usually pretty good. When I fail, it becomes evident, and affects not only me but the entire family.

In the third chapter of First Timothy, Paul discusses the qualifications for overseers and deacons. These are traits we should all aspire to have as husbands. With respect to the current topic, verses four and five say a husband "...must manage his own household well, with all dignity keeping his children submissive, for if someone does not know how to manage his own household, how will he care for God's church?" We must aspire to run our households well by taking care of it and nourishing it.

GOING THE EXTRA MILE

1. Scripture:
    a. Caring for the needs of others: Luke 10:25-37; James 1:19-27.
    b. Blessing to give: Acts 20:35.
    c. Managing your house well: 1 Timothy 3:5, 12; Titus 1:6-9.

2. The Bible clearly encourages us to care for the needs of others; it especially calls out caring for orphans, strangers, and widows.

It is therefore understandable when Paul says in 1 Timothy 5:8 that if we do not care for the needs of our family, and especially our wives, then we are worse than unbelievers. Consequently, in some denominational circles, if any neglect is serious enough, this Scripture might be cited essentially declaring the husband as an unbeliever, and therefore opening the door for justifiable divorce. Whether you agree with this or not, it is clear that taking care of your wife's needs – not wants – is of critical importance. What needs do you think your wife has that you might be neglecting? Explore this with her. You might think some of the things she says she needs might only be a want to you, and not very critical. However, it is not about you…it is about her. Figure out a few needs of your wife that you could do a better job meeting and put a plan in place to address them.

3. James Hunter's book *The Servant* states, "The role of leadership is to serve, that is, to identify and meet legitimate needs. In the process of meeting needs, we often will be called to make sacrifices for those we serve."[72] As husbands, we are also in a role of leadership. I encourage you to dissect this definition. Have you identified your wife's legitimate needs? How can you meet these needs? What sacrifices *must* you make to serve her effectively?

4. Chapter Five of *The Servant* is titled "The Environment." I would summarize this chapter as it relates to our topic: Husbands are responsible to meet the needs of their wives. This includes creating a healthy environment for her to grow and thrive. In spite

---

72 Hunter, *The Servant*, 85.

of the mass chaos, confusion, power politics, and other dysfunctions going on all around, husbands can still take responsibility for their little area [circle of influence] and make a difference. You might not be able to control the big picture, but you can control how you behave every day toward the people who have been entrusted into your care.[73] If a marriage were a garden, a husband would need to be constantly asking himself[74]:

    a.   What does my garden [wife] need?

    b.   Does our garden need to be fertilized with appreciation, recognition, or praise?

    c.   Does my garden need to be weeded?

    d.   Do I have pests to remove?

Consider your marriage and answer these questions.

---

73   Hunter, *The Servant*, 140.

74   Ibid., 134.

RULE NINE:

FLEE!

So flee youthful passions and pursue righteousness, faith, love, and
peace, along with those who call on the Lord from a pure heart.
2 Timothy 2:22

Flee! That is so hard for a man to do. Men from our American culture like to play at the edge of the cliff of sin, being deceived that sin is a black-and-white action. However, sin of action is always sin of the heart first. James says, "But each person is tempted when he is lured and enticed by his own desire. Then desire when it has conceived gives birth to sin, and sin when it is fully grown brings forth death" (James 1:14-15). Jesus says in Matthew 5:28, "[T]hat everyone who looks at a woman with lustful intent has already committed adultery with her in his heart."

This sin of the heart is especially true with pornography; many Christian men think they are clean, yet inside are corrupt[75]. The statistics are scary, almost 70% of church going men view porn on a regular basis, and over 50% of pastors do the same![76] Matthew 6:22 states,

---

75 Matthew 23:25. "Woe to you, scribes and Pharisees, hypocrites! For you clean the outside of the cup and the plate, but inside they are full of greed and self-indulgence."

76 Conquer Series, accessed April 29, 2017, https://conquerseries.com/set-free-stats/.

"The eye is the lamp of the body. So, if your eye is healthy, your whole body will be full of light, but if your eye is bad, your whole body will be full of darkness. If then the light in you is darkness, how great is the darkness!" Think about this: if you go to pornography or entertain adultery in your heart, it impacts your whole being, including your relationship with your wife. There is no choice but to set up good, safe boundaries and flee!

In my job, I discuss safety management every day. It is my job to focus on "near misses" – these are "almost injuries." The more effective my team is at reducing near misses, the less likely we will have a real injury, or even worse. To minimize risk of injury, we wear protective equipment and have clear, safe boundaries. We need to do the same for our marriages.

PORN STATS

- 76% of 18 to 24-year-old Christians actively seek out porn (Barna Group Survey, 2016).
- 71% of teens hide online behavior from their parents (Tru Research, 2012).
- 68% of church going men view porn on a regular basis (Pure Desire Ministries study, "Porn Usage in Evangelical Churches").
- 56% of divorce cases involved one partner having an obsessive interest in pornographic websites (American Academy of Matrimonial Lawyers, 2002).
- 54% of pastors view porn on a regular basis (Pure Desire Ministries study, "Porn Usage in Evangelical Churches").

From Conquer Series, accessed April 29, 2017,
https://conquerseries.com/set-free-stats

I often use the above analogy to illustrate the response to the following scenario: What kind of interaction am I "permitted" to have with a woman who is not my wife? This is, of course, the wrong question. I am looking at the line of "instant death" versus what is glorifying to God. It is like walking forward while looking back. Am I allowed to talk with a woman? Go to lunch with a woman? What if it is a business lunch? How about dinner or a movie? Can I share marriage problems with another woman? Can I go over to her house and "help her with something?" What about going into her bedroom? It would just be to fix something…or talk. Is it only when I take off my personal protective equipment, my clothes, then happen to trip and fall, and nine months later a baby miraculously appears, that it becomes sin? When we fail to set up safe boundaries for our interactions with other women we set ourselves up for a real injury to our marriage.

You Cannot NOT Think About Nothing.

When you have wandering sinful thoughts, the best way, and I believe the only way, you can make it go away is to fill your mind and heart with godly thoughts. These thoughts will push out the bad. It might take a while to get rid of those thoughts, but with purposeful effort (like changing where you are, what you are hearing, and what you are seeing), and prayer (c.f. Philippians 3:13-14; 4:4-9) these thoughts can be renewed in a more positive direction.

My personal boundaries might seem old-fashioned or strict, but I can tell you that they keep me from ever having to worry about having a bad trip or fall. In business, if I have to have a personal conversation with a woman, I try to do it in an open or public space; I have them in hallways or in a conference room with glass walls. I try to minimize my trips in cars alone or meals together. It is hard to avoid it 100% of the time, but I put out a lot of effort to minimize the risk. Away from work, I can count on one hand the number of times I have gone into a house with only a woman there – every time it was for less than five minutes and it was only because this woman needed real, immediate help. The whole time I was in the house I was in panic mode because I had crossed my boundary. In this situation, it is wise to invite someone to go in with you – even a child would be an effective safety net.

> **"Fatigue makes cowards of us all."**
> *Vince Lombardi.*
> When we are tired or weak, this is when we are the most vulnerable to sin and error. Be aware of this, and plan accordingly. Early in our marriage, my wife and I committed to not have conversations on sensitive topics after 8 o'clock at night. This worked wonders in our marriage. Ambrose Bierce said, "Speak when you are angry and you will make the best speech you will ever regret."

By nature, we like to push the limits, like a two-year-old who wants to touch a hot plate and continues to move his hand to touch it while looking back at the parent to see if it is okay. Instead, we need to guard our hearts and flee. For example, there is a safety regulation in the United States which requires people working within six feet (the conservative height of an average man) from the edge of the roof to be tied off with a harness. This way you can never "happen" to trip and fall off the edge of the roof.

Twice we are told in Malachi 2:13-16 to "guard yourselves in your spirit."

And this second thing you do. You cover the Lord's altar with tears, with weeping and groaning because he no longer regards the offering or accepts it with favor from your hand. But you say, "Why does he not?" Because the Lord was witness between you and the wife of your youth, to whom you have been faithless, though she is your companion and your wife by covenant. Did he not make them one, with a portion of the Spirit in their union? And what was the one God seeking? Godly offspring. So guard yourselves in your spirit, and let none of you be faithless to the wife of your youth. "For the man who does not love his wife but divorces her, says the Lord, the God of Israel, covers his garment with violence, says the Lord of hosts. So guard yourselves in your spirit, and do not be faithless."

Personally commit to guard your heart, soul, mind, and spirit. Set up clear, safe boundaries for yourself. If you have a problem with internet pornography, get accountability software put on all of your internet devices.[77] Just to clarify, a problem in this area would be defined as seeking and looking at pornography within the last year or even regularly once a year. Make a commitment to fill your eyes and heart with good and holy things instead of undesirable things; it is hard *not* think about something. We are instructed in 2 Timothy 2:22 not only to flee, but

---

77   CovenantEyes is one of the more popular and is used by my family. www.covenanteyes.org.

it tells us to pursue righteousness. Thus, we need to flee from the sin of our heart by pursuing good and godly thoughts. So when your mind wanders, find a pure thing to desire. If I see an attractive woman, I strive to replace her with my wife in my mind. Hebrews 13:4 says that the marriage bed is undefiled. So be biblical and "rejoice in the wife of your youth, a lovely deer, a graceful doe. Let her breasts fill you at all times with delight; be intoxicated always in her love" (Proverbs 5:18b-19). Furthermore, if you "[w]alk by the Spirit, you will not gratify the desires of flesh" (Galatians 5:16). There is a Cherokee proverb that says, "The one that wins is the one you feed." Which nature will you feed: Your old nature or your new nature?

GOING THE EXTRA MILE

1. Scripture:
    a. Flee: Proverbs 3:7-8; 4:15-16, 26-27; 5:8; 13:19; 14:7, 16; 16:17; 22:3; 27:8; 1 Corinthians 6:18; Psalm 34:14; 119:101, Matthew 5:29; 1 Corinthians 6:12.
    b. Garbage in, garbage out: Matthew 6:22-23; 1 John 2:15-17; Job 31:1.
    c. Focus on good things: Philippians 2:15a; 4:8; Proverbs 5:18-19.

2. We are clearly exhorted to guard our hearts, eyes, and minds. Job said, "I have made a covenant with my eyes; how then could I gaze at a virgin?" (Job 31:1). Yes, "All things might be lawful, but not all things are helpful" (1 Corinthians 6:12). What things can you

do to protect yourself? Make a commitment to share these with someone you trust to hold you accountable. Furthermore, I would recommend using a software app to help protect yourself from going to questionable websites on your computer and phone.

3. Peter encourages us in 1 Peter 5:8-9 to "[b]e sober-minded; be watchful. Your adversary the devil prowls around like a roaring lion, seeking someone to devour. Resist him, firm in your faith, knowing that the same kinds of suffering are being experienced by your brotherhood throughout the world." How could you apply this passage in your life? Write these actions down and commit to do them.

4. Clearly the statistics indicate that most men in the church struggle with sexually-related temptations and addictions. If you are one of these men, I would encourage you to find a group to help you address this and hold you accountable.

RULE TEN:

SERVE WITH YOUR WIFE:

Do we not have the right to take along a believing wife, as do the other apostles and the brothers of the Lord and Cephas?

1 Corinthians 9:5

The presumption with this rule is that you are already serving in your local church with your wife. You understand that we are *not* supposed to forsake the gathering together of believers (a.k.a. being active in your local church)[78], and as believers, we have a responsibility to build up and serve the church body.[79] However, if for some reason you are not active in your local church, please understand that you are neglecting an important part of your responsibility and sanctification as a believer.

Yes, our lives are busy: you work, your wife might work, your kids have school and activities, you need to make time for your marriage and family, and now I am saying you need to be engaged in church too? Yes! However, there is a way to have your cake and eat it too.

---

78 Hebrews 10:24-25. "And let us consider how to stir up one another to love and good works, not neglecting to meet together, as is the habit of some, but encouraging one another, and all the more as you see the Day drawing near."

79 1 Corinthians 12:7.

My wife and I have always been active in our local church. However, I learned the principle of serving together the hard way. Unfortunately, no one told me this principle; we figured it out much later in our marriage through much pain. I had been missing the opportunity to be with my wife while I was serving. Interestingly, of all the *Guy's Rules*, this is the only one I have not heard confirmed from another marriage resource.

A cheap date...

Dating can put more than a little strain on a budget, so it can be difficult to find something interesting to do together. Serving generally doesn't cost money. Some of the best times my wife and I have spent together has been through serving together. When we were dating, we used to run supplies to build houses from San Diego into Tijuana, Mexico, for houses for the poor. We spent many enjoyable hours together on someone else's dime... and it was constructive. Think about how you could date your mate while serving.

My wife and I have always had busy lives, but that didn't stop us from serving. When it came to ministry, we generally served apart rather than together. She was involved in women's ministry and children's ministry, and I was engaged in men's ministry. We were like ships passing in the night...for years. Our marriage suffered needlessly because of the choices we had made to serve apart. I do not remember how it happened, but during one of those many seasons of struggle, when there was little time left for our marriage, we both pulled out of the ministries we were engaged in and we started working with our local church's mission committee. My wife and I had been missionaries in Africa for four years, so we were uniquely qualified to serve together there. It was great; not only did it free up time for us, but now we were serving *together*, so our time together had this multiplying effect. Even the time commuting to and from church was a cherished moment alone. My wife is a great cook and often catered events at church, so I would become her very inadequate sous-chef or busboy. I was her Chief Servant – but we were together. When I was in seminary, Wendy was able to audit classes with me for free; she was there with me for all my biblical counseling classes as well as many others. She did all the reading too, so we could share much of the experience together. As it did in our marriage, this principle can have a significant, positive impact on your relationship as well.

Start looking at your local church and figure out which ministries fit you and your family. When the kids are younger, it might be children's ministry. When they are a little older, it could be setup for church or serving at a rest home. Furthermore, serving together as a family is a wonderful opportunity for your children to see your faith in action. If you have an opportunity to work with the poor, it gives them a better appreciation for what they have. Not only is serving together great family time, it is generally cheap. Most of you with young kids are also on a tight budget. You can often serve all day with little or no cost.

I would encourage you who are very engaged in men's ministry, or if your wife is heavily engaged in woman's ministry, that you prayerfully consider stepping back or even quitting. I am not saying you should avoid these ministries, as it is important to be with men and fellowship. I am talking about being engaged as a leader in separate ministries. Make a covenant between you and your wife to minimize all ministry activity away from each other; find something you can do as a team.

GOING THE EXTRA MILE

1. Scriptures:
    a. Be together: Deuteronomy 24:5; Ecclesiastes 4:12, 9:9; 1 Corinthians 7:5.
    b. One flesh: Genesis 2:22-24, Mark 10:7-9; 1 Corinthians 7:1-5.

2. In 1 Corinthians 6:14, Paul urges us to not be yoked with unbelievers. As couples, we should not be unequally yoked with spouses either. Think about it: if we are not going together at the same speed, strength, and direction, we will not be very effective. In your marriage, where are you unequally yoked? Think about things you could do to change this and commit to do them.

3. We are instructed in 1 Corinthians 7:5: "Do not deprive one another, except perhaps by agreement for a limited time, that you may devote yourselves to prayer; but then come together again, so that Satan may not tempt you because of your lack of self-control." Consider this verse and how it applies to the whole marriage

relationship. How much time should we be spending away from our spouses "except perhaps by agreement for a limited time, that you may devote yourselves to prayer?" Are you spending too much time away from your wife? What should change?

4. Create situations where you can be together and do things together. I love to bike – my wife not so much; but it is something we can do together, so she will do it, even though it might not be her favorite thing to do. Likewise, home improvement projects are not my favorite thing to do, but again, it is something we can do together. This helps us spend quality time together. Even though they might not be your favorite things to do, think about things you could do together and consciously make time to do them.

5. Consider going on a short-term mission trip together in a third-world context. If that sounds difficult, consider Mexico, it is not very far for many. If that is still not a legitimate option, try doing some disaster relief or working to help the homeless. If you have kids, find one where they can go and be engaged too. There are so many benefits to doing this. To name a few:
    a. Serving the Lord as a family together, outwardly focused versus self-focused, will change your family and give them an experience they will not forget.
    b. Serving with other believers closely together will be some of the best fellowship experiences you will ever have.
    c. If you are serving people less fortunate than yourselves, it will change your world view and increase you and your family's gratefulness. Your family will experience something most first-world people will ever see.

If you are fortunate enough to take advantage of serving people less fortunate than yourself, figure out how you can remain engaged with these people. One thing I highly recommend is personally supporting a missionary overseas. Neal Pirolo's book, *Serving as Senders*[80], is a great resource to help figure out how to do this.

---

80 Neal Pirolo, *Serving As Senders Today* (San Diego, CA: Emmaus Road International, 2012).

RULE ELEVEN:

THE BUCK STOPS WITH YOU

For the husband is the head of the wife even as Christ is the head of the church, his body, and is himself its Savior.
Ephesians 5:23

This is where we wrap it all up. As husbands, God calls us to be the leader in our marriage relationship. Everything the marriage does, or fails to do, is our responsibility. We are required to demonstrate and reflect the same character God shows us by being merciful, gracious, slow to anger, and abounding in steadfast love and faithfulness[81] to our wives. This is not easy.

Honestly, I struggled with this early in my marriage. It was only a few months after my wife and I got married that we were seeking help from a Christian counselor. It helped some, but the first thing that really hit home with me was a book by Gary Smalley titled, *If Only He Knew.* I found it very practical. It taught me what I could do to make the woman I love feel better about the husband

---

81 Exodus 34:6-7. "The Lord passed before him and proclaimed, "The Lord, the Lord, a God merciful and gracious, slow to anger, and abounding in steadfast love and faithfulness, keeping steadfast love for thousands,[a] forgiving iniquity and transgression and sin, but who will by no means clear the guilty, visiting the iniquity of the fathers on the children and the children's children, to the third and the fourth generation."

she chose to live her life with. The book contained a few questionnaires which my wife and I worked through that helped me figure out what was important to my wife; I posted these results on my truck dash to keep me on task. However, the most lasting thing I learned from this book was that I was responsible for the marriage. Gary Smalley had discovered after years of marriage counseling that:

> If a couple has been married for more than five years, all of the husband's emotional unhappiness is 100 percent his fault.[82]

Basically, he was saying that if your wife is *coocoo* you will figure that out within five years; otherwise, if she is willing to put up with you that long, she is committed and only you, by your actions or inactions, could drive her away. Wow! Think about it...you are responsible for one hundred percent of your marriage results! That's powerful! Consequently, you need to take ownership of your marriage. This is one reason God made us the head and the leader. The ball is in our court. But there is hope, because after depending on the Lord we do not have to depend on anyone else to make our marriage better. It is between God and you.

However, we must admit that our wives carry a significant amount of influence in our lives. In the movie *My Big Fat Greek Wedding*, the mother gives her daughter

---

82 Smalley, *If Only He Knew*, 95.

advice about being a wife and says, "The man is the head, but the woman is the neck, and she can turn the head any way she wants." As I said earlier, as the husband we own all that our family does or fails to do. Yes, even if they influence us. Ensure you are not like Ahab who unfortunately was completely influenced by his wife. Even though he really was king of his castle and Israel, he all but abdicated his responsibility of leadership to his wife, Jezebel. It says in 1 Kings 21:25-26 that, "There was none who sold himself to do what was evil in the sight of the Lord like Ahab, whom Jezebel his wife incited. He acted very abominably in going after idols, as the Amorites had done, whom the Lord cast out before the people of Israel." Thus, independent of our wives and their influence, we are accountable for leading our marriage.

As a leader, our position can be a lonely place. In fact, Elizabeth Elliot said, "Loneliness is a required course for leadership." Why? Because at times you have the weight of all that your family does or fails to do on your shoulders... alone. When the buck stops with you, and everyone is leaning on you to carry the family through, then there is no one for you to lean on other than the Lord. You must be the man your family can lean on as you lean on Him. This is similar to what Paul says in 1 Corinthians 11:1, "Be imitators of me, as I am of Christ."

Another way it can be lonely as a leader is in our speech. There are times when it is wise not to tell your wife the whole story. She needs you to be a rock of security in her life. I have been laid off three times in my life, so any hint of bad news about work can contribute to her worrying unnecessarily. I have learned not to overshare about the struggles I have at work. I have learned that if work is difficult and I feel the need to share, it needs to be with someone else other than my wife. Like I said, it can be lonely as the leader.

I have often been told, "My wife and I share everything. We keep no secrets." I have learned that this is neither wise nor kind. Sometimes being brutally honest is just brutal. For example, if you are struggling with pornography, running to your wife to share your struggles is *not* recommended. Get help, and when you get it under some type of control, then share with her. Otherwise, each time you share your struggles, it is like committing adultery again and again…it is cruel.

When you have difficult topics to discuss, ensure your wife is in the best state of mind to receive it. It is often lonely while you wait to share, however this is a biblical principle. Solomon speaks about this in Ecclesiastes 3:7b, saying that there is "a time to keep silence, and a time to speak." He also discusses this principle in the following Proverbs:[83]

| Proverbs 10:19 | When words are many, transgression is not lacking, but whoever restrains his lips is prudent. |
| Proverbs 10:21 | The lips of the righteous feed many, but fools die for lack of sense. |

---

83 Note: Appendix A has a more complete list of Proverbs that helped me in all my daily interactions with my wife and others for over twenty-five years.

Proverbs 12:16	The vexation of a fool is known at once, but the prudent ignores an insult.
Proverbs 12:23	A prudent man conceals knowledge, but the heart of fools proclaims folly.
Proverbs 18:2	A fool takes no pleasure in understanding, but only in expressing his opinion.
Proverbs 21:23	Whoever keeps his mouth and his tongue keeps himself out of trouble.

Yes, he states in Proverbs 27:5 that "Better is open rebuke than hidden love." My point is that there is a time and a place for everything. Thus, when it is wise to hold your tongue, it will not be easy, and can be lonely.

During passionate conversations, or as my brother and his wife call it "intense fellowship," while others sometimes call them arguments – make a commitment to attack the problem and not the person...the character of your wife. Be passionate *and* respectful *and* constructive; do not to use labels or declarative statements like, "You're an idiot," or "That was the stupidest thing I have ever heard." Paul tells us in Ephesians 4:29 to "[w]atch the way you talk. Let nothing foul or dirty come out of your mouth. Say only what helps, each word a gift" (MSG). Let us ensure our words are truly a gift to our wives.

Another part of being an effective leader in life and marriage is being a reader. Former President Harry Truman said, "Not all readers are leaders, but all leaders are readers." I would argue this starts with reading your

Bible regularly. Another way to own your marriage is to read about marriage and leadership in general. The books in the bibliography are all books which have had a significant constructive impact on my life and marriage. Some of them are secular books, some are both Christian and secular, and some are written completely from a Christian perspective. They had a positive impact on me and how I lead, both at work and at home. I did not always agree with everything written in them, especially the last portion of Victor Frankl's book on *Man's Search for Meaning*[84]. My wife always says, "Eat the meat, and spit out the bones." I expect that if you filter the secular books from a Christian perspective, as we should with all of life, then they will have a positive impact on you also.

"Find a way or make one."
Hannibal.

Have the tenacity of Hannibal to make your marriage work. If one way doesn't work, figure out another. Pray always and "cast your cares upon Him" in the process (1 Peter 5:7). Take charge of what will enhance your relationship, what will make her feel loved, what will promote harmony, and own the spiritual development and direction of your family...no excuses.

---

84 With respect to Victor Frankl's book, *Man's Search For Meaning*, his ultimate goal through his life experiences is to introduce logotherapy, a method of counseling others to give people meaning in their lives. The first seventy-five percent of the book talks about his experiences and his suffering, then how he and others responded to it. This is very enlightening. When he starts getting into how he uses this to counsel, from a Christian perspective it misses the mark. Though the principle that we need meaning in our lives is true, but as a Christian, I recognize these can only permanently be found in God and not in the temporary things of this life.

Many of you might not be readers or feel you do not have the time to read. I have recently discovered another alternative: listening to audiobooks and recorded sermons. There are many apps that enable you to do this for free. I am as busy as the next guy, however, in the past six months, I have been able to listen to over twenty audiobooks as well as listen to the entire Bible. I did almost all of this commuting or while doing chores around the house.[85] As I have mentioned before, multitasking is key to getting the most out of your short time here on earth.

In the end, the buck stopping with us is in the choices we make. Every day we have a choice to be the Chief Servant or to be selfish, to become the plaything of our environment or to be a light, to confess the sins of our wives or love them in word and deed. We can choose to focus on the perceived wrongs and injustices done to us or make decisions to love our wives and love the Lord. Ultimately, to have the best marriage possible, we must be the leader and own our marriages, and we must make our relationship with the Lord paramount. God's Word must be our guide in our life and marriage. Read it regularly and meditate on it. Grow closer to Him, know Him, and love Him. If the Lord is first in our life[86], we know everything else will fall into place.

---

85 *Hoopla* and *Overdrive* are both great smartphone applications. Both are free and only require a library card. *Hoopla* has a lot of Christian titles.

86 Matthew 22:37b-38. "You shall love the Lord your God with all your heart and with all your soul and with all your mind. This is the great and first commandment."

After putting the Lord first, your next priority is protecting and guarding your marriage, understanding that you are responsible to remember that, "What therefore God has joined together, let not man separate" (Mark 10:9), and that your wife is "your companion by covenant."[87] *The Guy's Rules* discussed in this devotional are only a tool to help your marriage. I hope the lessons I learned the hard way will help you grow closer to your Lord and to your bride.

GOING THE EXTRA MILE

1. Scriptures:
    a. Greatest commandment: Matthew 22:36-40; Deuteronomy 6:5.
    b. Commit your way to the Lord: Psalm 37:3-5; 55:22; Proverbs 3:3-12; 16:3.

2. The great wise man Walt Disney said, "When your values are clear decisions are easy." I have found this principle to be true in all areas of life. Furthermore, I have discovered that the converse is true too: "If decisions are hard, then your values are NOT clear." Thus, evaluate what is truly of value in your life. Matthew 6:21 says, "For where your treasure is, there your heart will be also." Think about where your treasure is. What are your values? My wife and I have encouraged couples to write down what is truly important in their marriage.

---

87 Malachi 2:14b. "[T]he Lord was witness between you and the wife of your youth, to whom you have been faithless, though she is your companion and your wife by covenant."

102

Then when problems and issues come up, they can reference the family values. It takes away the power struggle by appealing to an agreed upon, neutral set of rules. Commit to write down your personal values, roles, and goals. Furthermore, work with your wife to write down your shared family values, roles, and goals.

3. Ponder the passages in this chapter regarding the words that come out of your mouth. How can you be much more constructive in the words you use? Are you sharing or talking when silence and listening would be better? Consider James 1:19-21 from *The Message*. How could you apply this in your marriage?

> Post this at all the intersections, dear friends: Lead with your ears, follow up with your tongue, and let anger straggle along in the rear. God's righteousness doesn't grow from human anger. So throw all spoiled virtue and cancerous evil in the garbage. In simple humility, let our gardener, God, landscape you with the Word, making a salvation-garden of your life.

4. Hunter says, "Anyone who ever said marriage was 50/50 probably wasn't married very long."[88] If you are not 100% committed to making your marriage work, as though its success is 100% dependent on you, then your marriage is in trouble. Make a commitment here and now to live as if 100% of your marriage's success depended on your ownership through God's help and support. Remember what Jesus says in John 15:5b, "for apart from me you can do nothing."

---

88 Hunter, *The Servant*, xvii.

5. As I stated previously, to have a successful marriage you *must* have God at the center of your life and your relationship. What can you do to ensure He is the center of your life? I would encourage you to meet regularly with other husbands to ensure you stay on track and to hold you accountable. As mentioned in Rule ONE, the book *Practicing His Presence*[89] is a great place to start.

6. Consider Ephesians 5:25 where we are encouraged to love our wives as Christ loved the church and gave Himself up for her. This means that Christ's love for the church MUST be a reflection and a model on how we act as husbands toward our wives. Considering this, apply this principle in light of the following:

   - Not only did He give Himself up by dying for us, but He gave Him-SELF up for the church. i.e. He became selfless and emptied Himself for the church, so we ought to do this for our wives as well.

   - Christ didn't come to be served but to serve [c.f. Matthew 20:28]. As mentioned before, be the Chief Servant.

   - "When we were still sinners Christ died for us [Romans 5:8]." In other words, in spite of how she acts, we must act lovingly and die to ourselves.

---

89 Brother Lawrence and Frank Laubach. *Practicing His Presence* (Jacksonville, FL: The SeedSowers, 1973).

- Christ came to reconcile us to God [c.f. Romans 5:10]. i.e. We should not only be the Chief Servant, but the Chief Reconciler in our relationship.

- Christ will never leave or forsake the church [c.f. Hebrews 13:5]. Can you imagine Christ divorcing or forsaking His bride? It should be just as absurd for a husband to act this way towards his wife.

Think of three things you could do in light of this principle and apply it. Tell a friend to help hold you accountable.

BIBLIOGRAPHY

Adams, Jay E. *Christian Living in the Home*. Phillipsburg, NJ: P&R, 1972.

Covey, Stephen R. *The 7 Habits of Highly Effective People*. New York, NY: Fireside, 1989.

Driscoll, Mark and Grace. *Real Marriage: The Truth about Sex, Friendship and Life Together*. Nashville, TN: Thomas Nelson, 2012.

Frankl, Victor E. *Man's Search for Meaning*. New York, NY: Simon & Schuster, 1984.

Hunter, James C. *The Servant*. New York, NY: Crown Business, 2012.

Mack, Wayne A. *Strengthening Your Marriage*. Phillipsburg, NJ: P&R, 1977.

Scott, Susan. *Fierce Conversations*. New York, NY: The Berkley Publishing Co., 2004.

Smalley, Gary. *If Only He Knew*. Grand Rapids: Zondervan, 2012.

SELECTED PROVERBS TO HELP YOUR MARRIAGE

Below are verses from Proverbs which have been on my desk at work for over twenty-five years to remind me to think about my all my interactions.

Proverbs 9:8	Do not reprove a scoffer, or he will hate you; reprove a wise man, and he will love you.
Proverbs 9:10	The fear of the Lord is the beginning of wisdom, and the knowledge of the Holy One is insight.
Proverbs 10:8	The wise of heart will receive commandments, but a babbling fool will come to ruin.
Proverbs 10:17	Whoever heeds instruction is on the path to life, but he who rejects reproof leads others astray.
Proverbs 10:19	When words are many, transgression is not lacking, but whoever restrains his lips is prudent.
Proverbs 10:21	The lips of the righteous feed many, but fools die for lack of sense.

Proverbs 11:2 — When pride comes, then comes disgrace, but with the humble is wisdom.

Proverbs 11:12 — Whoever belittles his neighbor lacks sense, but a man of understanding remains silent.

Proverbs 12:1 — Whoever loves discipline loves knowledge, but he who hates reproof is stupid.

Proverbs 12:15-16 — The way of a fool is right in his own eyes, but a wise man listens to advice. The vexation of a fool is known at once, but the prudent ignores an insult.

Proverbs 12:18 — There is one whose rash words are like sword thrusts, but the tongue of the wise brings healing.

Proverbs 12:23 — A prudent man conceals knowledge, but the heart of fools proclaims folly.

Proverbs 13:2 — From the fruit of his mouth a man eats what is good, but the desire of the treacherous is for violence.

Proverbs 13:16 — Every prudent man acts with knowledge, but a fool flaunts his folly.

Proverbs 14:6 — A scoffer seeks wisdom in vain, but knowledge is easy for a man of understanding.

Proverbs 16:32 — Whoever is slow to anger is better than the mighty, and he who rules his spirit than he who takes a city.

Proverbs 17:10 — A rebuke goes deeper into a man of understanding than a hundred blows into a fool.

Proverbs 17:27 — Whoever restrains his words has knowledge, and he who has a cool spirit is a man of understanding.

Proverbs 18:2   A fool takes no pleasure in understanding, but only in expressing his opinion.

Proverbs 21:23   Whoever keeps his mouth and his tongue keeps himself out of trouble.

Proverbs 26:4   Answer not a fool according to his folly, lest you be like him yourself.

Proverbs 26:11-12   Like a dog that returns to his vomit is a fool who repeats his folly. Do you see a man who is wise in his own eyes? There is more hope for a fool than for him.

Proverbs 26:17   Whoever meddles in a quarrel not his own is like one who takes a passing dog by the ears.

Proverbs 27:5   Better is open rebuke than hidden love.

Proverbs 27:14   Whoever blesses his neighbor with a loud voice, rising early in the morning, will be counted as cursing.

BUILD A BRIDGE TO HAWAII...

This is one of my favorite marriage jokes. It would not be so funny if there were not any truth in it.

> A man walking along a California beach was deep in prayer. Suddenly, the sky clouded above his head and, in a booming voice, the Lord said, "Because you have *tried* to be faithful to me in all ways, I will grant you one wish."
>
> The man said, "Build a bridge to Hawaii so I can drive over anytime I want." The Lord said, "Your request is very materialistic. Think of the enormous challenges for that kind of undertaking. The supports to the bottom of the Pacific! The concrete and steel it would take! It will nearly exhaust every natural resource I have made. I can do it, but it is hard for me to justify your desire for worldly things. Take a little more time and think of something that would honor and glorify me."

The man thought about it for a long time. Finally, he said, "Lord, I wish that I could understand my wife. I want to know how she feels inside, what she's thinking when she gives me the silent treatment, why she cries, what she means when she says nothing's wrong, and how I can make a woman truly happy."

The Lord replied, "You want two lanes or four on that bridge?"

Cary Dennis[90]

---

90 Thrifty Fun, Accessed July 4, 2017, http://www.thriftyfun.com/tf427287.tip.html.

SOME OF BURNER'S FAVORITE MOTIVATIONAL QUOTES

I have always been a fan of quotes. I often find them thought provoking and convicting. Below are some of my favorites that I have collected over the years that pertain to life as a husband.

Burner's Top 5:

When your values are clear, decisions are easy.

– Walt Disney

If you ever wrap your emotional life around the weaknesses of another person you have empowered those weaknesses to control you.

– *The 7 Habits of Highly Effective People*, Stephen Covey

The successful person has the habit of doing the things failures don't like to do…They don't like doing them either necessarily. But their disliking is subordinated to the strength of their purpose.

– From an essay titled "The Common Denominator of Success", E.M. Gray

In the work place, employees will spend roughly half their waking hours working and living in the environment you create as the leader. I am amazed at how nonchalantly and even flippantly people respond to the responsibility. There is a lot at stake and people are counting on you...

> – *The Servant*, James C. Hunter

For the leader [husband], there is no trivial comment. Everything each of us says leaves an emotional wake... positive or negative. Take responsibility for your emotional wake.

> – *Fierce Conversations*, Susan Scott

Communication:

People don't care how much you know until they know how much you care.

> – Theodore Roosevelt

You communicate all the time, but most of it is without words.

> – *Cross-Cultural Connections*, Duane Elmer

We are always communicating, verbally and non-verbally. Therefore, we must be vigilant, aware of how and what we are communicating.

> – *Cross-Cultural Connections*, Duane Elmer

What you are shouts so loudly in my ears I cannot hear what you say.

> – Ralph Waldo Emerson

If it's important to that person, then it's important. So go there.

> – *Fierce Conversations*, Susan Scott

Be here, prepared to be nowhere else...speak and listen as if this is the most important conversation you will have with this person. It could be. Participate as if it matters. It does.

> – *Fierce Conversations*, Susan Scott

Spiritual:

I have got so much to do today that I need to spend
another hour on my knees praying.

– Martin Luther

Decisions and Actions:

There are two primary choices in life; to accept conditions
as they exist, or accept responsibility for changing them.

– Denis Waitley

Experience is not what happens to you. It's what you do
with what happens to you.

– Aldous Huxley

It's not what happened to you in life, it's what you do
about it.

– W. Mitchell

Not making a decision is itself a decision. Not making
a choice is itself a choice.

– Søren Kierkegaard, Danish Philosopher

Perfection is not attainable, but if we chase perfection
we can catch excellence.

– Vince Lombardi

Keep in mind that you are always saying "no" to
something.

– *The 7 Habits of Highly Effective People*, Stephen Covey

Though no one can go back and make a brand new
start, anyone can start from now and make a brand new
ending.

– Carl Bard

If you don't take control of your life, don't complain
when others do.

– Beth Mende Conny

Your feelings of respect must be aligned with your
actions of respect.

– *The Servant*, James C. Hunter

Sometimes when I consider what tremendous consequences come from little things, I am tempted to think there are no little things.

– Bruce Barton

"Patience" is doing something you don't want to do for a long time – with joy.

– Unknown

Failure is not fatal, but failure to change might be.

– John Wooden

An apology does not require humility, asking for forgiveness does.

– Burner paraphrase

Love:

To love you as I should, I must worship God as Creator. When I have learnt to love God better than my earthly dearest, I shall love my earthly dearest better than I do now. In so far as I learn to love my earthly dearest at the expense of God and instead of God, I shall be moving towards the state in which I shall not love my earthly dearest at all. When first things are put first, second things are not suppressed but increased.

– C.S. Lewis

Love is not affectionate feeling, but a steady wish for the loved person's ultimate good as far as it can be obtained.

– C.S. Lewis.

LISTENING TO YOUR WIFE

A paraphrase of "Ministry of Listening"
from *Life Together* by Dietrich Bonhoeffer[91]

The first service that one owes his wife consists of listening to her. Just as love to God begins with listening to His Word, so the beginning of love to our spouse is learning to listen to her. It is God's love for us that He not only gives us His Word but also lends us His ear. So it is His work that we do for our wives when we learn to listen to them. The Christian husband so often thinks he must always contribute something when his wife is speaking[92], that this is the one service he has to render. He forgets that listening can be a greater service than speaking.

Our wives are looking for an ear that will listen. Too often they do not find it from their husbands because he is talking when he should be listening.[93] But he who can no longer listen to his wife will soon be no longer listening to God either; he will be doing nothing but prattling in the

---

91 Dietrich Bonhoeffer, *Life Together* (New York: HarperCollins, 1954), 97-99.

92 Proverbs 18:2. "A fool takes no pleasure in understanding, but only in expressing his opinion."

93 Proverbs 10:19. "When words are many, transgression is not lacking, but whoever restrains his lips is prudent."

presence of God too. This is the beginning of the death of the spiritual life, and in the end, there is nothing left but spiritual chatter and clerical condescension arrayed in pious words. One who cannot listen long or patiently will presently be talking beside the point and never really be speaking to his wife, albeit he be not conscious of it. Any husband who thinks that his time is too valuable to spend keeping quiet will eventually have no time for God or his wife, but only for himself and for his own follies.

Biblical husbandly stewardship and care are more than speaking the Word, it is also the obligation of listening. There is a kind of listening with half an ear that presumes already to know what your wife is going to say.[94] It is an impatient, inattentive listening, that despises your wife when you are only waiting for a chance "for the husband to speak," and thus shut her down. This is no fulfillment of this obligation for the husband, and it is certain that here, too, your attitude towards your wife reflects your relationship to God. It is little wonder that we are no longer capable of the greatest service of listening that God has committed to us, that of hearing our wives on lesser subjects.

> But he who can no longer listen to his wife will soon be no longer listening to God either; he will be doing nothing but prattle in the presence of God too.

Secular education today is aware that often a person can be helped merely by having someone who will listen to them seriously, and upon this insight it has

---

94   Proverbs 18:13. "If one gives an answer before he hears, it is his folly and shame."

constructed its own soul therapy, which has attracted great numbers of people, including Christians. But Christians have forgotten that the ministry of listening has been committed to them by Him who is Himself the great listener[95] and whose work they should share.[96] **We should listen with the ears of God that we may speak the Word of God.**

---

95 Psalm 66:17-20; Proverbs 15:17; 1 Peter 3:12, 5:7; 1 John 5:14-15.

96 James 1:19b. "[L]et every person be quick to hear, slow to speak, slow to anger."

ANGER

Anger is NOT in itself sinful. It is an emotional response to a perceived injustice. It can be good or bad. Gary Chapman said, "Anger was designed to be a visitor, never a resident."

Have a plan on how to deal with anger. It is not a question of "if" you will be angry, but "when."

> The Lord is merciful and gracious, slow to anger and abounding in steadfast love.
> – Psalm 103:8

> Fathers, do not provoke your children to anger, but bring them up in the discipline and instruction of the Lord.
> – Ephesians 6:4

> Know this, my beloved brothers: let every person be quick to hear, slow to speak, slow to anger; **For the anger of man does not produce the righteousness of God.**
> – James 1:19-20

> But the fruit of the Spirit is love, joy, peace, patience, kindness, goodness, faithfulness, gentleness, self-control; against such things there is no law.
> – Galatians 5:22-23

Beloved, *never* avenge yourselves, but leave it to the wrath of God, for it is written, "Vengeance is mine, I will repay, says the Lord."

– Romans 12:19

Refrain from anger, and forsake wrath! *Fret not yourself;* it tends only to evil. For the evildoers shall be cut off, but *those who wait for the Lord shall inherit the land.*

– Psalm 37:8-9

Whoever is slow to anger has great understanding, but he who has a hasty temper exalts folly.

– Proverbs 14:29

Good sense makes one slow to anger, and *it is his glory to overlook an offense.*

– Proverbs 19:11

Be angry and do not sin; do not let the sun go down on your anger, and give no opportunity to the devil.

– Ephesians 4:26-27

Let all bitterness and wrath and anger and clamor and slander *be put away from you,* along with all malice. Be kind to one another, tenderhearted, forgiving one another, as God in Christ forgave you.

– Ephesians 4:31-32

A soft answer turns away wrath, but a harsh word stirs up anger.

– Proverbs 15:1

Be not quick in your spirit to become angry, for anger lodges in the bosom of fools.

– Ecclesiastes 7:9

A fool gives full vent to his spirit, but a wise man quietly holds it back.

– Proverbs 29:11

Whoever is slow to anger is better than the mighty, and
he who rules his spirit than he who takes a city.
> – Proverbs 16:32

A hot-tempered man stirs up strife, but he who is slow
to anger quiets contention.
> – Proverbs 15:18

But now you *must put them all away*: anger, wrath…
> – Colossians 3:8a

A man of quick temper acts foolishly, and a man of evil
devices is hated.
> – Proverbs 14:17

And the Lord said, "Do you do well to be angry?"
> – Jonah 4:4

A man without self-control is like a city broken into
and left without walls.
> – Proverbs 25:28

If a wise man has an argument with a fool, the fool only
rages and laughs, and there is no quiet.
> – Proverbs 29:9

A man of wrath stirs up strife, and one given to anger
causes much transgression.
> – Proverbs 29:22

Love is patient and kind; love does not envy or boast;
it is not arrogant or rude. It does not insist on its own
way; **it is not irritable or resentful…**
> – 1 Corinthians 13:4-5

The **vexation of a fool is known at once, but the
prudent ignores an insult.**
> – Proverbs 12:16

Be angry, and do not sin; ponder in your own hearts
on your beds, and be silent. Selah.
> – Psalm 4:4

But I say to you that everyone who is angry with his brother will be liable to judgment; whoever insults his brother will be liable to the council; and whoever says, 'You fool!' will be liable to the hell of fire. So if you are offering your gift at the altar and there remember that your brother has something against you, leave your gift there before the altar and go. First be reconciled to your brother, and then come and offer your gift.

– Matthew 5:22-24

Note: Emphases added by the author.

For more on dealing with anger see Gary Chapman's book, *Anger: Taming a Powerful Emotion.*

FORGIVENESS

by Brett Burner

Some years ago, I was reeling with a pretty great offense that was done to me. It was the kind of thing that happened over several years, involving a betrayal of trust from someone who had been a friend and leader. It was a hurt that ran deep and left many scars, and it had left me fairly bitter and resentful over the matter. As a Bible teacher and lover of Jesus, this is never a good addition to having a successful Christian walk.

One day while counseling with a trusted mentor, he asked me: "Is there anything that he might feel you owe him an apology for?"

My hackles rose. "What? No! Of course not! I don't owe *him* an apology!"

"You didn't hear me," he said. "I said, 'Is there anything that he might *feel* you owe him an apology for?'"

Still defensive, I rolled my eyes and sarcastically quipped, "Sure...he might *FEEL* I do, but I don't! *He* owes *me* an apology!"

"If he feels you have offended him, you have to ask for forgiveness." He was staring at me.

"Why should I ask for forgiveness when he is the one who hurt me?" This wasn't fair.

"Because even if he *feels* offended, you need ask him to forgive you for it. And then you need to forgive *him*." I felt like I was falling. Down and endless pit. In the dark. Alone.

"But what if I don't forgive him? Because right now, I really don't."

"You have to," he responded. "Paul wrote that we are to forgive others as God forgave you" (Ephesians 4:32).

"Okay…"

"How much were you forgiven?" he asked.

I felt very small. "Everything…"

"So how much should you forgive?"

Sigh. I didn't want to answer. But I did. "Everything."

And the fact is, I didn't deserve my forgiveness. It is grace that was given to me. I didn't earn it. I did nothing special for it. Freely given, freely give…

"Okay…I need to forgive him." But ever the pragmatist: "But what if I don't FEEL forgiveness in my heart? Doesn't God want me to be genuine?"

He shook his head. "God wants you to be *obedient*. How you *feel* about it doesn't matter."

"Okay," I offered, "but what if I forgive him, and then tomorrow I don't?"

He said, "That's not forgiveness. That's emotion. Forgive him, or don't. But it's not how you feel about it. That's on you."

"So if I forgive him today, but I'm angry about it tomorrow…"

"That's your problem…not his."

Thus began a three-week conversation on forgiveness. We met each week (and served together during the week) and continued the discussion. I got it. God wanted me to both ask for forgiveness, and to forgive. But I wanted to reconcile it in my heart. To understand it. I would do it… truly, my life, my spiritual life, even my other relationships, in many ways my future in ministry, depended on it.

I was no longer fighting it…I was on a quest of insight into this mystery of God.

Then one day…it hit me. Hard. Full revelation. I had a debt that was owed to a bank. And it was *forgiven*.

Here is how I present this principle now, with a group of people, or, more often, to a hurting individual sitting across from me:

I pull out my wallet and pull out a bill. I prefer a twenty, though it can be a dollar. The higher the bill, the better. (This demonstration has to cost me, and the more value in this sacrifice, the better the impact.) I ask: "Whose money is this?"

"It's yours" they will say.

Next, I hand it to them. I ask: "Now, whose money is this?"

They say, "It's still yours."

"Okay. Now place the money in your pocket. All the way. Or even better, into your wallet."

This is always a point of hesitation, but they do it. If they don't, I wait until they comply.

I declare: "We both agree that you are currently in receipt of my $20. If I were to ask for it back, you agree that it is mine. So you are currently 'in debt' to me for $20."

They agree.

Then I ask, "Are you ready? This is the best part." I pause. It usually makes me emotional, because this is a powerful moment.

Then I say simply: "I forgive you."

At this point, they are usually scrambling to give me my money back. But in truth, it is no longer mine.

If other people are looking on, I include them. "Everyone here has now become my witnesses. You were previously in debt to me for $20, but now you are forgiven. I have written off that debt. You owe me nothing."

I continue: "And it doesn't matter how I feel about it. Forgiveness is a *legal transaction*. My emotions don't matter. I might feel bad about it tomorrow. I might need that money. I might wish I still had it. But your forgiveness has been legally declared. If I try to take you to court saying you still owe me a debt, all these people could come and declare witness that they heard me offer forgiveness. I have no legal grounds to try to get that money back. If I am angry, that's my problem. Forgiveness was already given."

And now the point: When someone offends you, they have taken something from you. They have hurt you, wounded you. They *owe* you. That's why we say, "You *owe* me and apology." We *see* them as having a debt to us.

But we owed a debt to God. It was a debt we couldn't pay. It was a debt of sin…my sin. I offended God. I hurt him, wounded him. I sent him to the cross, where *he* paid my debt. I am forgiven. And therefore, I must forgive others, as God has forgiven me.

"But I am still hurt!" you say. Yes, it hurts. And that is for you to look to God to heal your wounds, not to others. Forgiveness doesn't mean approval. It doesn't mean you condone what they did. It doesn't mean the relationship will necessarily even be restored, or that trust will be established. But when you forgive, you give up your right to hold the value of that debt on someone else. Then you are free to give your attention to God, who, now that you have released that debt to which you held so tightly, is now free to minister to your soul. And as you grow, you will learn to let the pain go. You will learn that his "grace is sufficient for you" (2 Corinthians 12:9), which means that your salvation (His grace) is all that you need (sufficient). That it is good enough that you are saved. That our sufferings are *not even worth a comparison* to the glory that will be given to us (Romans 8:18). That he has poured out such an extravagant blessing upon us in our salvation that we are to be called his sons and daughters (1 John 3:1).

That is the importance of forgiving others.

One thing that is always interesting to me: whenever I finish this demonstration, they always try to give me the money back. That's because we all have a problem *receiving* forgiveness. I never let them. I tell them that to do so would take away the power of the truth they had just been shown. I ask, "Why are you trying to give me your money?" Once a woman kept trying to slip the money back to me. She really couldn't accept *being* forgiven. She finally found my wife and told her she wanted to give her some money. My wife asked: "Did my husband just talk to you about forgiveness? I can't accept that money." My wife is awesome.

To round out the story, the following week after my conversations on forgiveness, I sat down and wrote out a letter to the man who had hurt me. I asked him for forgiveness for anything I might have done. I told him I forgave him, even if it was my own perceptions. I thanked him for having been in my life and for the lessons he had benefited me with.

Easiest letter I've ever written.

THE GUY'S RULES: CONDENSED VERSION

Rule ZERO: The Pagan Guy's Rules:
- "Everyone did what was right in his own eyes."
  – Judges 21:25b.

- Three reasons this is RULE ZERO:
  1. It adds no value.
  2. It will not help you.
  3. It is useless.

- Unfortunately, Rule ZERO is the most common rule husbands follow.

  » By nature, we are selfish and put ourselves first.

Rule ONE: In the Beginning, God...:
- "In the beginning, God created..." – Genesis 1:1a.

- God must be the beginning of all things, including marriage. The first commandment tells us, "You shall have no other gods before me" (Exodus 20:3).

- God must be first, everything else comes later.

  » Yes, your wife comes later.

Rule TWO: BEFRIEND Your Wife:
- "It is not good that the man should be alone."
  – Genesis 2:18.

- "Two are better than one, because they have a good reward for their toil. For if they fall, one will lift up his fellow. But woe to him who is alone when he falls and has not another to lift him up!" – Ecclesiastes 4:9-10.

- "Happiness is being married to your best friend."

- When your marriage is built upon a foundation of friendship coupled with a joint Christ-centered relationship, everything else just seems to come easier; it softens the edges of the hard times, trials, and tribulations.

Rule THREE: Work on Your 10%...Let God Deal with the Rest

- "First take the log out of your own eye, and then you will see clearly to take the speck out of your brother's eye." – Matthew 7:5b.

- People feel like others are the bigger part of any relationship problem.

- At the same time, most would admit that they are at least part of the problem…even if it is only 10%.

- Marriages are not any different. You think your spouse is the bigger part of the problem and she probably feels the same way about you.

- Does it really matter who is more at fault?

  » After you figure out who is responsible for their appropriate allocation of the blame, you still have to work on your part and she has to work on her part.

- Ultimately, you both own 100% of your own personal sanctification through abiding in the Lord.

- Too often we are so focused on, or even consumed by, the wrong or perceived wrong that our wife has done to us that we cannot focus on anything else, much less our own sanctification.

> » "Anytime, we think the problem is 'out there,' that thought is the problem." –Stephen Covey.

- In the end, our duty is to rely on the Lord to work on your wife.

  > » You trusted Him to save you and take your sins away, you can at least trust Him to work in your wife's life.

  > » You cannot control her; you must let God change her heart.

  > » Even if you are only 10% of the problem, *you must own 100% of your part,* then pray for your wife and ask God to deal with her heart, whether she changes or not.

Rule FOUR: Be the Chief Servant...and Lead:

- "Whoever would be great among you must be your servant, and whoever would be first among you must be slave of all." – Mark 10:43b-44.

- Many men think and act like being the husband makes them the supreme commander. This is one perspective...and one-sided, and it is certainly not a holistic biblical perspective.

- In Ephesians 5:25, men are instructed NOT to "rule" their wives, but to *love* them "as Christ loved the church and gave [H]imself up for her." The question we have to ask as husbands is, "Are you reflecting the love of Christ to your wife as He does for the church?" Think about it, you are called to be a model of the same love that Christ has for us.

- Jesus, in Mark 10:45, says regarding leadership: "Whoever would be first among you must be slave of all. For even the Son of Man came not to be served but to serve, and to give His life as a ransom for many."

- Jesus clearly calls leaders to be servants. Thus, He is calling husbands not to be lords of the family, but to be the servant leader of the household. Thus, the biblical attitude of the husband must be that of Chief Servant of the home.

Rule FIVE: LOVE is a VERB:

- "Husbands, love your wives [with an affectionate, sympathetic, selfless love that always seeks the best for them] and do not be embittered or resentful toward them [because of the responsibilities of marriage.]" – Colossians 3:19 AMP.

- Biblical love is *not* a feeling, it is a verb.

  » Husbands are called to love their wives in action and deed.

  » It has been said, "love is as love does."

  » We might have the best intentions, but if our actions do not align with them it means nothing. Our actions must align with our intentions.

- Christian love is generally defined using 1 Corinthians 13:1-8a. Notice that this passage is all about what you do and not feelings – it is unconditional agape love.

- Men are responsible and able to choose to love (the verb) their wives in all circumstances.

Rule SIX: Leave and CLEAVE:

- "Therefore a man shall leave his father and his mother and hold fast [cleave] to his wife, and they shall become one flesh." – Genesis 2:24.

- After Creation, the first thing God deals with is the relationship of the man and the woman…marriage.

- The husband is supposed to <u>leave</u> his parents and <u>cleave</u> to his wife.

  » *Leave your parents*: You are a new family unit and your wife is now the number one human in your life. Not your parents, your extended family, and not your children.

- **The husband-wife relationship is designed to be permanent, as long as you both shall live.**

  - The parent-child relationship is temporary.

» *Cleave to your wife*:

- She is now the number one woman in your life.

- She is the queen and must be treated like this.

- Cleaving is more than being attracted to your wife, though this is an important and foundational biblical principle of marriage.

  - Cleaving to your wife means that you recognize that you are incomplete without her.

  - Cleaving is actively and purpose-fully guarding your relationship and holding fast to her.

Rule SEVEN: UNDERSTAND Your Wife:

- "Likewise, husbands, live with your wives in an under-standing way, showing honor to the woman as the weaker vessel, since they are heirs with you of the grace of life, so that your prayers may not be hindered." – 1 Peter 3:7.

- Do you want your prayers hindered?

  » If we do not live with our wife in an under-standing way, our prayers will be hindered.

» To understand a wife well, it requires the husband to put her needs above his.

» The fifth habit of Stephen Covey's *The 7 Habits of Highly Effective People* is to "Seek first to understand, then to be understood."

• Understanding your wife is more than listening.

• Figure out what she is actually communicating.

  ▪ This takes effort and conscious thought.

  ▪ More than just the words, but tone and body language.

  ▪ As Covey says, "Listen with your eyes."

» Furthermore, women generally are more feelings-oriented.

  ▪ We show honor to our wives by not reacting directly to what they say or feel.

  ▪ Listen with empathy.

Rule EIGHT: Provide for the NEEDS of your Wife:

• "But if anyone does not provide for [the *needs* of] his relatives, and especially for members of his household, he has denied the faith and is worse than an unbeliever." – 1 Timothy 5:8.

» This would definitely include our wives.

» Too often I know I do not take this responsibility seriously.

• This is more than just meeting material needs, but it starts there.

» Are you providing for your wife's spiritual and emotional needs?

» *Needs* and *wants* are very different things.

> » We regularly need to step back, look at the big picture, and identify the ever-changing needs of our wives.

- The husband is responsible to create a proper *environment* for his wife and children to thrive in.

- Think about the farmer. He does not make the plants grow, that is God's job. The farmer is responsible to create the best conditions for the crop to grow and thrive.

- Likewise, the husband has the same responsibility. The crop of a farmer needs constant attention and so do our wives.

Rule NINE: FLEE!

- "So flee youthful passions and pursue righteousness, faith, love, and peace, along with those who call on the Lord from a pure heart." – 2 Timothy 2:22.

- Flee! This is so hard for a man to do.

  > » Men from our American culture like to play at the edge of the cliff of sin, being deceived that sin is a black-and-white action.

  > » Sin of action is always sin of the heart first.

- This sin of the heart is especially true with pornography; many Christian men think they are clean, yet inside they are corrupt.

- The statistics are scary:

  > » About 70% of church-going men view porn on a regular basis

  > » Over 50% of pastors do the same.

- Matthew 6:22 states, "The eye is the lamp of the body. So, if your eye is healthy, your whole body will be full of light, but if your eye is bad, your whole body will be full of darkness. If then the light in you is darkness, how great is the darkness!"

> » Think about this: If you go to pornography or entertain adultery in your heart, it impacts your whole being, including your relationship with your wife.

> » There is no choice but to set up good, safe boundaries, and flee!

- Twice we are told in Malachi 2:13-16 to "guard yourselves in your spirit."

> » Commit to guard your heart, soul, mind, and spirit.

> » Set up clear, safe boundaries for yourself.

- There is a Cherokee proverb that says,

> » "The one that wins is the one you feed."

> > ▪ Which nature will you feed? Your old nature or your new nature?

Rule TEN: Serve WITH your Wife:

- "Do we not have the right to take along a believing wife, as do the other apostles and the brothers of the Lord and Cephas?" – 1 Corinthians 9:5.

- If your lives are busy, serving together will have a significant and positive impact in your marriage.

> » Even the time commuting to and from the place you serve can be a cherished moment alone.

Rule ELEVEN: The Buck Stops with YOU:

- "For the husband is the head of the wife even as Christ is the head of the church, his body, and is himself its Savior." – Ephesians 5:23.

- God calls us to be the leader in our marriage relationship.

- Everything the marriage does, or fails to do, is our responsibility.

- We are required to demonstrate and reflect the same character God shows us by being merciful, gracious, slow to anger, and abounding in steadfast love and faithfulness to our wives.

  » This is not easy.

- To have the best marriage possible, you must be the leader and own your marriage.

  » You must make your relationship with the Lord paramount.

    ▪ Start by taking God's Word seriously and using it to guide your life.

      ♦ Read it regularly and meditate on it to grow closer to Him, to know Him, to love Him.

      ♦ If the Lord is first in your life, everything else will fall into place.

- Your next priority is protecting and guarding your marriage.

  » You are responsible to remember that, "What therefore God has joined together, let not man separate" (Mark 10:9).

  » Do everything in your power to ensure you don't "separate."

ABOUT THE AUTHOR

Michael Burner has a Master of Theological Studies with a concentration in Biblical Counseling from the Reformed Presbyterian Theological Seminary in Pittsburgh, Pennsylvania. He has been walking with the Lord for over thirty-four years, married for thirty years, and has four adult children who are walking with the Lord all through God's grace.

Michael was a Marine Corps Officer, has over twenty years of corporate leadership experience, and was a missionary in Kenya with his family for four years. Throughout  this period, he and his wife, Wendy, have been active members of the churches they attended, including regularly providing biblical counseling for couples and individuals, as well as serving in other relationship ministries.

For questions and more information about *The Guys Rules*, Michael can be reached at Michael.GuysRules@gmail.com.

44801980R00092

Made in the USA
Middletown, DE
10 May 2019